Applied Tarot

An Excessively Practical Guide to Tarot
Card Interpretations

by Emily Paper

Applied Divination
Redmond

Copyright © 2020 Emily Paper

All rights reserved. No portion of this book may be reproduced or utilized in any form, or by electronic, mechanical, or other means, without the prior written permission of the publisher.

Published by Applied Divination

ISBN 978-1-7356170-1-5
Library of Congress Control Number: 2020944822

Front cover image by Emily Paper
Illustrations by Emily Paper
Photographs from Unsplash.com
Book design by Emily Paper

First printing edition 2020

Applied Divination
www.applieddivination.com
info@applieddivination.com

Contents

Introduction 1
   How did this come about?............... 1
   How to use this book................... 2
   Reversals.............................. 3
   About the Deck in this Book............ 5
The Major Arcana 6
The Minor Arcana 98
   What are the Minor Arcana?............ 99
   Sentence Combinations Calculator...... 100
   Wands................................. 108
   Cups.................................. 151
   Swords................................ 194
   Pentacles............................. 237
Image Credits 280
Acknowledgements 280
About the Author 283

Introduction

How did this come about?
I lost my keys. It wasn't anything more profound than that, just lost keys.

I looked everywhere, frustrated not only by the missing keys, but moreover by the fact that this was normal behavior for me. My spouse teased me for it, but he too was frustrated with me. Often, I would take *his* keys when I had misplaced my own. Then I would promptly misplace his as well.

In a fit of frustration, I grabbed a random deck of tarot cards[1] and three cards dropped out:
The reversed King of Pentacles
The upright Six of Cups
The upright Seven of Swords

Peculiar.

For myself, the reversed King of Pentacles is about smashing the Patriarchy - it is something I try to do on a day to day basis, so the reversed king appearing in a reading is not new to me.
Unfortunately, smashing the patriarchy alone does not help one find their keys.

The Six of Cups typically has something to do with a child. Did one of my offspring take my keys?

---

[1] my tarot decks are strewn about the house haphazardly, don't judge

The reversed King *describing* the Six of Cups made me think about my daughter. She's a female-presenting adult (the reverse of a King) but also my child (the Six of Cups)

Now, what of the Seven of Swords, a card meaning thievery and mischief?

I found my keys in a jacket I had borrowed[2] from her.

Then I started thinking - If the tarot cards can so explicitly and plainly find my keys for me, what else might they do?

Rather than offer the mysterious, contemplative, and theoretical musings that your typical Tarot reading gives, this book is filled with practical, direct and *applied* answers for each card.

Where did *you* lose *your* keys? Let the Tarot cards tell you!

How to use this book
Think of this book as a reference, not a novel. You do not need to read it front to back, nor should you. This book is for answering basic questions with individual tarot cards, and assumes you have a tarot deck on hand.[3]

---

[2] I stole it. I stole my daughter's jacket. It was very seven of swords of me.
[3] If you do not own a Tarot Deck, here are a couple of starter suggestions: *The Rider Waite* - this is the classic Tarot deck with familiar iconography.
The Golden Tarot - a simple deck to learn, it's similar to the Rider Waite, but the symbolism and details are easier to remember.

Steps:
1. Ask your question.
2. Shuffle the deck and pull a card.
3. Skip to the page for the card pulled, and hopefully you will get some functional insight.

If you *do not* get any functional insight, you can attempt a wordier answer by using the Combinations calculator on Page 100.

Finally, understand that if the individual card interpretations don't help, or the combinations calculator spews randomness, your question might not have a simple answer and you might need to figure things out on your own. Good luck with that!

A quick note on movie recommendations: A good movie falls into several themes, so take my suggestions lightly. These are all movies that are fairly well known, that I have personally seen, and that fit the card category listed. Do not be offended by my movie choices - (For example, I prefer MCU over DC and you might be different although I do not understand how that is possible!)

I thought about doing book recs too, but that would take a whole other book.

If you have movie or book recommendations, contact me through www.emilypaper.com

Reversals
In a genuine tarot reading, an upside-down card can be just as important -if not more so- as a card that is right side up. I use reversed cards in almost all my in-depth readings.

However, the interpretation of reversals is so involved and dependent upon the individual question, I have chosen not to include the meanings here. This book is intended to be an extremely simplistic view of each card. Introducing reversed interpretations would upset any straightforward answer.

Tarot readers who are comfortable with obfuscation can always choose to read the reversals, of course. Here are a few relatively simple ways to incorporate reversals:

1. Interpret the cards as the opposite of an upright meaning. For example, if you are looking for something to eat and draw The Empress upright, she would tell you to choose whole, natural foods. A reversed Empress might suggest you pick the most unnatural and processed item you can find.

2. Interpret the cards as being more intimate or localized to you. For example, if you are looking for a place to travel and draw the Knight of Wands upright, in this book it suggests you go to a car race in Indianapolis. A reversed interpretation might be to watch a derby in your hometown, instead.

3. Interpret the card with a more negative meaning (or positive if the card upright is traditionally negative.) For example, if you were wondering what part of your house to clean and you drew the Ace of Pentacles, upright it suggests you water your plants. A reversed interpretation might be to pull weeds, instead. The object is still taking

care of plants, it is just a bit dirtier and less fun.

4. Interpret it as a look back at the preceding card in the deck. For example, if you draw the reversed Six of Pentacles (generosity), check the meaning of the Five of Pentacles (impoverishment) and realize that perhaps you are not the giver in the six, but the receiver.

I do mention a few reversed meanings in this book, but an in-depth interpretation should be saved for another tome.

About the Deck in this Book

The US copyright owner for the Rider-Waite wanted money for the classic RW iconography, but I'm too stubborn and cheap for that. Instead, I created my own cards with similar imagery, using gorgeous photos from Unsplash.com.

This deck will become available for purchase on emilypaper.com as soon as I figure out how to do that. I do not think there is a Tarot card that explains how to publish a deck, but who knows - I have not explored all practical interpretations yet.

Photographer names are listed at the back. Go check out their work! Thanks Unsplash!

The Major Arcana

0

The Fool

The fool is a new beginning. The baby bounds happily out of the sandbox, toward whatever mysteries are on the other side.

The Fool

The fool dances through the hilltops without direction, his faithful pup by his side. Blissfully unaware of the danger, the fool is poised to fall with the very next step.

However, that is just what we see when we look at the card. What we do not know is what is on the other side of that leap. The fool card asks us to take a risk and make the jump. Trust yourself.

If you were truly about to make a terrible mistake, your dog (or another trusty companion) might notice and warn you.

Questions answered by the Fool:

Who? A young person with his or her head frequently in the clouds
What? A new venture
Where? Somewhere new and unfamiliar
When? Immediately; January and February
Why? Because without risks and challenges, there is no growth
Yes or No? Yes

What should I clean?
- The baby's room
- The litter box or pet's area

Where are my keys?
- On a ledge somewhere

The Fool as:

An action
- Try something new
- Take your dog for a walk
- Adopt a pet!

Place in your house?
- A high location, such as a shelf or balcony
- Upstairs

Place in your city?
- Somewhere you have never been
- A dojo
- A children's museum

Place in the world?
- The Himalayas
- The Alps
- The Rocky Mountains

Something to eat?
- Bananas
- Avocados

A color? White, Yellow

A movie theme? Taking a chance or a fresh start
- Sleepless in Seattle
- Alice Doesn't Live Here Anymore

A new career?
- A startup or seed company
- Something in the tech industry
- Working with pets

Some Fool combinations

With Judgment: A person has an overwhelming urge to follow their heart.
With Seven of Wands: A person defends their outrageous new idea - it is good!
With Ace of Cups: A free spirit falls in love.
With King of Swords: An otherwise disciplined worker starts a completely new career.
With Eight of Pentacles: A graduating student takes their first leap into a new career.

Before any card: A new beginning regarding (card)
After any card: A fresh start, a bold risk

The Major Arcana represent significant, unchangeable life events.
The Fool could indicate:

- A new baby
- Changing careers
- Moving houses
- An engagement or wedding
- A precarious hike up a mountain

I

The Magician

The Magician possesses all the tools and wisdom needed to complete the task. What is the next move? This magician already knows.

The Magician

The Magician is the all-knowing, all powerful person. The Magician has every tool they need readily at their fingertips. The Magician can conjure and create worlds.

The magic here is not mysterious, extraordinary, or fantastical, it is a practical application of reality. The Magician tells us to use the tools we already have to accomplish our task.

Our tools might be something we *know*, something we *have*, or something we *are*.

Questions answered by the Magician:

Who? Someone who knows a remarkable amount for her or his age or position; someone with a surprising talent; an actual magician
What? The use of an old skill in a new way
Where? An interesting shop you have never visited
When? Very soon; May and June; August and September
Why? Because you already have the skills you need
Yes or No? Yes

What should I clean?
- Organize your tools
- Your home office

Where are my keys?
- The tool box
- On your desk

The Magician as:

An action?
- Learn a magic trick
- Fix something broken
- Start a project

Place in your house?
- The office
- The kitchen
- A crafts area
- The workshop

Place in your city?
- A magic shop
- The library
- A craft store
- The office

Place in the world?
- Egypt
- Ireland
- India
- Haiti

Something to eat?
- Blueberries
- Garlic
- Chocolate
- Superfoods

A color? Aquamarine, blue, yellow

A movie theme? Magic, or already possessing the skills needed to win
- The Prestige
- The Martian
- Now you See Me
- Slumdog Millionaire

A new career?
- Magician
- Construction
- Network architecture
- Communications

Magician combinations

With Sun: Hard work and willpower leads to immense joy.
With Four of Wands: A dream is manifested at home; a home renovation project.
With Two of Cups: A partnership leads to successful business; creating strong bonds through hard work.
With Knight of Swords: A skilled person jumps into a career and finds instant success.
With Seven of Pentacles: You already possess the tools you need to reap great success this year; diligence will pay off.

Before any card: You have all the tools you need to obtain   (card)
After any card: Mastery of a subject, resourcefulness

The Major Arcana represent significant, unchangeable life events.
The Magician could indicate:

- A skilled person, such as a professor or specialist coming into your life
- A life event requiring significant resources or knowledge
- A first glimpse of your future destiny
- A magic trick

The High Priestess

The High Priestess is wise beyond years, solving issues from within not out. The baby is cloaked in wisdom and mystery.

The High Priestess

The High Priestess is intuitive and looks inside for the truth, rather than seeking answers from outside. The High Priestess is replete with knowledge of the world and can sense the direction that a certain path will take.

The Priestess is a teacher, guide, or wise source of psychic information.

Questions answered by the High Priestess:

Who? Your own subconscious; a wise woman
What? You already know something, but you do not realize you know it; follow your dreams
Where? Delphi; Fatima or Lourdes; Macedonia; In your own head
When? At night; During the new moon; June and July
Why? You know why
Yes or No? You know the answer

What should I clean?
- The tub or shower
- The blinds

Where are my keys?
- In a chair
- Near a window

The High Priestess as:

An action?
- Do some introspection
- Meditate
- Practice yoga
- Take a nap and record your dreams

Place in your house?
- The living room
- The bedroom

Place in your city?
- A yoga studio
- A University
- A therapist's office

Place in the world?
- Tibet
- Costa Rica
- Indonesia
- Kenya

Something to eat?
- Whatever you are craving
- Eggs
- Green tea

A color? turquoise, blue, Indigo

A movie theme? Intuitive wisdom, mystery
- Arrival
- Willow
- Hidden Figures

A new career?
- Psychologist
- Conflict resolution
- Psychic or intuitive healer
- Detective

High Priestess combinations

With Moon: Try meditation or hypnosis
With Ace of Wands: Intense meditation leads to a new start or new career. The drive comes from within.
With Three of Cups: Your friends know what is best for you - ask them.
With Queen of Swords: An intelligent person trusts herself and creates clear boundaries.
With Six of Pentacles: Spiritual insight is bestowed upon someone in need.

Before any card: Trust your intuition about (card)
After any card: Wisdom, intuition

The Major Arcana represent significant, unchangeable life events.
The High Priestess could indicate:

- A message from a psychic
- A gut feeling you cannot shake
- A fleeting thought you should not ignore
- Robes

The Empress

The Empress is the all-knowing mother. The baby is filled with an abundance of nurturing and creative energy.

The Empress

The Empress is the Earth Mother. She has the biggest and most compassionate heart, and often gives so much and suffers greatly for it.

The Empress warns us not to bite off more than we can chew, but when we do take on a project, fulfill it to the end with immense love, practical wisdom, and empathy for others.

Questions answered by the Empress:

Who? a Mom; a mother figure; a grandmother figure; mother earth
What? A garden
Where? Mom's house; a garden; a rocking chair
When? When the baby is born (literal or metaphoric); The beginning of Spring; The beginning of Autumn
Why? Because everyone needs a little bit of compassion and empathy, even you
Yes or No? Yes

What should I clean?
- The living room
- The nursery

Where are my keys?
- Mom has them

The Empress as:

An action?
- Care for someone
- Adopt a pet
- Have a baby

Place in your house?
- The dining room
- Kitchen projects
- The crafts closet
- A rocking chair

Place in your city?
- School
- Supermarket
- Hospital

Place in the world?
- Scandinavia
- Canada
- Western Europe
- Australia

Something to eat?
- Lasagna
- A grilled cheese sandwich
- Something homemade and filling
- Natural, whole grain foods

A color? Green, turquoise, orange

A movie theme? Nature, motherhood
- The Joy Luck Club
- March of the Penguins
- Akeelah and the Bee

A new career?
- The care industry or hospitality
- A work from home job
- Nanny or babysitter
- Mom

Some Empress combinations

With Star: A strong intuitive feeling of destiny being fulfilled; A pregnancy.
With Ten of Wands: The burden of parenthood or caregiving.
With Four of Cups: Someone is apathetic about nature or global warming.
With Page of Swords: A young person is curious about fertility, such as a student in a sex ed class.
With Five of Pentacles: Poverty is aided by a mother's love. Seek a parent for help with one's needs.

Before any card: Nurture (card)
After any card: Creativity, the Earth, a Mother's love

The Major Arcana represent significant, unchangeable life events.
The Empress could indicate:

- A pregnancy or adoption
- An environmental phenomenon
- A significant event involving a mother figure
- Something that affects planet Earth
- A plant

IV

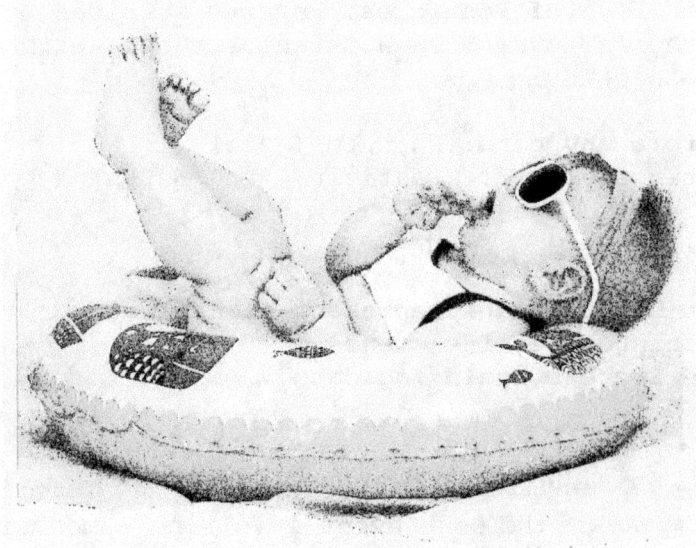

The Emperor

The Emperor is an all-knowing and kind leader, but also authoritative. The baby sits upon his throne with status and material wealth.

The Emperor

The Emperor is the Father figure or authority. He favors rules and regulations and expects everyone to follow them. Because he is diligent and educated, the Emperor is a wise, skillful and stable counsel to seek.

He is a great boss or father, or merely a strong masculine influence.

Questions answered by the Emperor:

Who? a Dad; a Grandfather; a professor; a masculine boss
What? The need to set limits and become more stable
Where? A dad's house. A workplace
When? Unexpectedly abrupt; The start of Spring; Aries
Why? Because when you do not have the answers, you must find the person who does
Yes or No? Yes, if you follow the rules

What should I clean?
- The office
- The front hall

Where are my keys?
- On the desk
- Near the table
- Dad has them

The Emperor as:

An action?
- Ask an expert
- Lead the team

Place in your house?
- The bathroom (The Thinker on the Throne!)
- The big comfy chair in the living room
- The desk chair in the office

Place in your city?
- A University
- A lecture hall
- The Police station

Place in the world?
- Washington DC
- Berlin
- The capital of a country

Something to eat?
- Steak and potatoes
- A burger
- A giant cold mug of beer
- A shot of whiskey

A color? Red, purple, orange

A movie theme? Authority, a Patriarch
- The Godfather
- The Hunt for Red October
- Three Men and a Baby

A new career?
- Self-employment
- Government job
- Entrepreneurship

Some Emperor combinations

With Tower: A violent war.
With Nine of Wands: The resistance against authority, such as a child standing up to a Dad.
With Five of Cups: An authority figure grieves a loss.
With Ten of Swords: A powerful structure begins to collapse; The smashing of the patriarchy.
With Four of Pentacles: A Dad tries to help; ask your father.

Before any card: An authority figure is involved in (card)
After any card: Structure, power

The Major Arcana represent significant, unchangeable life events.
The Emperor could indicate:

- A new boss or career reorganization
- A message from an authority
- Wisdom obtained through reading or study
- An executive's chair

V

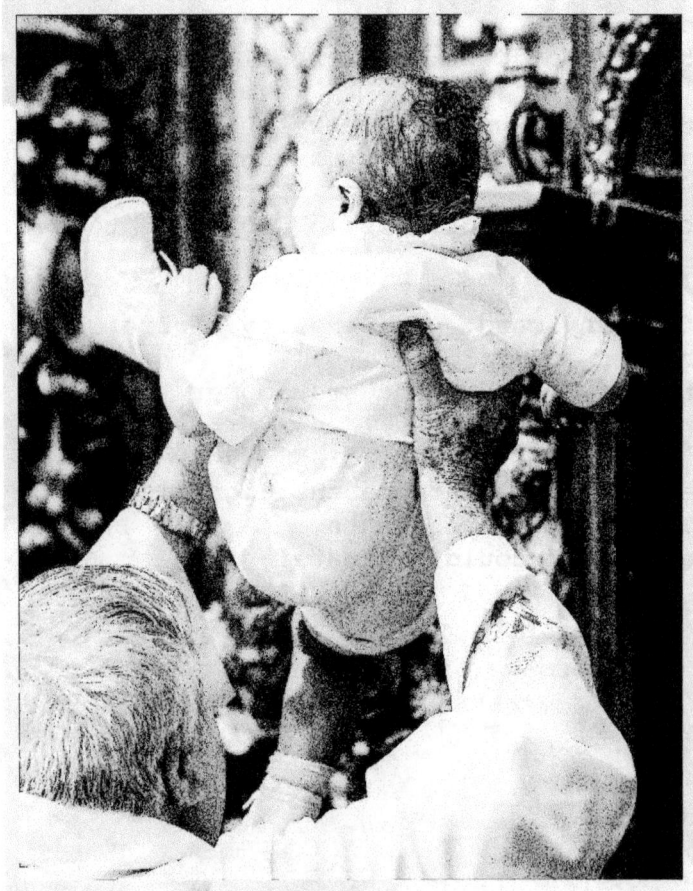

The Hierophant

The Hierophant is about tradition, business, and conformity. This hierophant is all ceremony, but for what purpose?

The Hierophant

The Hierophant follows rules from an established tradition, possibly ones created years ago by a strict and authoritative patriarchy. The Hierophant is akin to a priest and is the embodiment of these established doctrines. This may be a curse, a blessing, or both.

Sometimes sticking to our values and beliefs is what pulls us through novel situations. However, sometimes the Hierophant is a warning that we should reconsider what we value the most.

Questions answered by the Hierophant:

Who? A religious leader; a teacher; a police officer
What? Traditional guidance
Where? A church; a pew; the establishment
When? April and May; When traditions are followed
Why? Because sometimes you just need to follow the rules
Yes or no? Maybe, it depends

What should I clean?
- The shrine
- Religious or traditional iconography
- Heirlooms

Where are my keys?
- They are with god now (ha, just kidding!) maybe with religious things
- Where you usually locate them

The Hierophant as:

An action?
- Pray to the gods
- Obey the rules
- Follow tradition

Place in your house?
- A meditation space
- Under spiritual icons, such as a cross hanging in your living room

Place in your city?
- The church
- A big business headquarters

Place in the world?
- The Vatican
- Mecca
- Fatima
- Jerusalem

Something to eat?
- Meat and Potatoes
- Fish on Fridays
- Matzo balls

A color? turquoise, violet, brown

A movie theme? Big business, religion
- Dogma
- A Christmas Carol
- Silicon Valley (TV, HBO)

A new career?
- Pastor
- Librarian
- Bookkeeper or Accountant
- Teacher

Some Hierophant combinations

With the Devil: Heaven and Hell are one. The establishment is unraveling.
With Eight of Wands: A quick decision is made based on morality or ethics.
With Six of Cups: A child obeys the rules.
With Nine of Swords: The rules are causing a lot of anxiety, perhaps they are too strict.
With Three of Pentacles: Conform to the desires of the team; a morale building exercise.

Before any card: A traditional approach to (card)
After any card: Institution, religion, doctrine

The Major Arcana represent significant, unchangeable life events.
The Hierophant could indicate:

- Strict rules and regulations
- An institution, such as a church or large company
- A religious figure or book
- A church wedding

VI
The Lovers

The Lovers are values aligned and the optimal mix of logic and passion. Here, it is also a wonderful relationship.

The Lovers

The Lovers card is often confused as a foretelling of love and relationship. It is not so direct that it means true love with unicorns and rainbows (although it *could* mean that, if the question asked was "Is this true love with unicorns and rainbows?")

Rather, the Lovers represents a perfect blend of the head and heart; it could be the moment of an epiphany, when the thing you need to know suddenly comes to you in a spark of inspiration.

But yes, for the romantic at heart, it also means love, partnership, connection, and sex.

Questions answered by The Lovers:

Who? Your romantic partner; Yourself at your highest good
What? A connection
Where? Your bed; A church; Your lover's house
When? May to June; Gemini astrological sign; Quickly; At first sight
Why? Happiness comes when the head meets the heart
Yes or No? Yes

What should I clean?
- The bedroom
- The place where you do your best work

Where are my keys?
- Your partner has them

The Lovers as:

An action?
- Do something romantic
- Do something that inspires you

Place in your house?
- The bed
- The couch or love seat

Place in your city?
- A theatre
- The park
- The beach

Place in the world?
- Paris
- The Tropics
- Virginia ("Virginia is for Lovers")

Something to eat?
- Oysters
- Figs
- Almonds
- Fajitas for two

A color? Pink, crimson

A movie theme? Love, an alignment of values or ideals
- The Princess Bride
- When Harry Met Sally

A new career?
- Advertising and communications
- Any job involving a partner

Lovers combinations

With Temperance: A relationship is rewarding.
With Six of Wands: A partnership is recognized.
With Seven of Cups: A daydream about love.
Eight of Swords: One partner feels imprisoned.
With Two of Pentacles: The partners must adapt to new changes.

Before any card: The lovers or partners must deal with (card)
After any card: Values alignment, love

The Major Arcana represent significant, unchangeable life events.
The Lovers could indicate:

- A marriage
- A relationship
- A business partnership
- One's values
- A heart

VII

The Chariot

The Chariot is about action and direction, but it will not move until you tell it to. This baby will choose a direction a bit later.

The Chariot

The Chariot sounds like it means charging ahead with full force, but it is more about pausing to think about which direction you will take, and *then* going full steam ahead.

In traditional imagery, the two lions in front of the Charioteer are not moving, but they are perched and ready to take off at a moment's notice.

The Chariot is that split second before the decision is made. Neither option is the wrong one, so do not be afraid to choose.

As the motto says, "Just do it."

Questions answered by the Chariot:

Who? Your auto mechanic; the driver of your next Lyft car; an Equestrian
What? Endurance
Where? The tracks; the garage
When? A new moon; nighttime; June and July
Why? "Procrastination is the thief of time" - Edward Young; bite the bullet and choose your next path
Yes or No? Yes, if you go for it

What should I clean?
- The car

Where are my keys?
- The car

The Chariot as:

An action?
- Go for a drive
- Choose

Place in your house?
- The main entrance
- Your garage

Place in your city?
- The bus terminal
- The racetrack
- The highway out of town

Place in the world?
- Germany
- Heathrow Airport
- Le Mans
- The Indianapolis Motor Speedway

Something to eat?
- Nutrition bar
- A sandwich
- A milk shake
- Fast food

A color? Red

A movie theme? Travel, decisions, races
- Cars
- The Matrix
- Run Lola Run

A new career?
- Race car driver!
- Transport driver, long haul trucker, or dispatcher
- Networking
- Quality control

Some Chariot combinations

With Death: The wrong decision.
With Five of Wands: A good decision leads to healthy competition.
With Eight of Cups: All choices are abandoned.
Seven of Swords: This path requires some deviance or trickery.
With Ace of Pentacles: A new job opportunity requiring some travel.

Before any card: Make a decision about (card)
After any card: Travel; direction; going for it

The Major Arcana represent significant, unchangeable life events.
The Chariot could indicate:

- A new job or life direction
- A new car
- A decision to make
- A literal chariot

VIII

Strength

Strength is courage, patience and mind over matter. It tells us to feel the fear and do it anyway. The baby is in control.

Strength

The Strength card is about your inner will, confidence, and the animalistic nature that is inside all of us. In its simplest form, the Strength card also recognizes our fight or flight instinct. Neither fight nor flight is the incorrect reaction, as they exist to save our lives.

The Strength card tells you to use your inner reserves in the matter at hand.

Questions answered by Strength:

Who? Your personal trainer; a zoologist; a veterinarian
What? Your inner reserves; your most basic instincts; survival
Where? The gym
When? July-August; During sunny weather
Why? Because sometimes when we spend an hour on our most basic needs, it inspires our brain into more logical action
Yes or No? Yes, if you are strong enough

What should I clean?
- Exercise equipment
- The cat's litterbox

Where are my keys?
- On the treadmill or wherever you work out
- Near your pet

Strength as:

An action?
- Go for a run
- Have sex
- Eat a hearty meal

Place in your house?
- The fitness area or gym equipment
- The bedroom
- The shower

Place in your city?
- The gym
- The park
- Your favorite restaurant

Place in the world?
- Boston
- Alaska
- Scotland
- Strongman, Olympics, or another competition

Something to eat?
- A protein bar
- Fruit from a tall tree
- An animal you killed and cooked yourself

A color? Red, lavender

A movie theme? Strength, inner reserves
- Gladiator
- The Hunger Games

A new career?
- Veterinary or human medicine
- Human Resources
- Manual Labor

Strength combinations

With World: Great fulfillment comes from within.
With Three of Wands: Expanding a business requires immense bravery.
With Nine of Cups: Focus.
Six of Swords: Have strength to move on and get out of a difficult situation.
With King of Pentacles: A compassionate person provides security.

Before any card: Have confidence about (card)
After any card: Strength, conviction, pets

The Major Arcana represent significant, unchangeable life events.
Strength could indicate:

- A situation requiring willpower
- Exercise
- A pet
- A lion

IX

The Hermit

The Hermit represents an ascension to a higher
plane. The baby withdraws for study,
introspection, and their own self-guidance.

The Hermit

The Hermit lives alone high in the mountains, with nothing but a lamp and a powerful mind.

The Hermit is alone, but not lonely. The constant processing of a highly intellectual mind is great company.

When the Hermit card is pulled, it is a time for inner reflection away from the hustle and bustle of the outside world. Thoughtful introspection will uncover the solutions to your questions.

Questions answered by the Hermit:

Who? An accountant; a boss or mentor; a therapist; your oldest child
What? A retreat
Where? In a dark space; high on a mountain
When? August-September; after some thought; soon
Why? Because the answers you seek are within you, so stop asking these cards
Yes or No? Maybe - you will have to think about this issue yourself

What should I clean?
- The bathroom

Where are my keys?
- The bathroom
- The last place you were alone

The Hermit as:

An action?
- Think first
- Get away for a bit
- Rest

Place in your house?
- The bookshelf or library
- The place where you can be alone to think and dream

Place in your city?
- The outskirts of town
- Nearby caves or viewpoints

Place in the world?
- The mountains
- Switzerland
- A silent retreat

Something to eat?
- Fatty fish
- Nuts and seeds
- Coffee
- Brain food

A color? Magenta, indigo, violet, grey

A movie theme? Wisdom, introspection, solitude
- Wild
- Koyaanisqatsi
- The Truman Show

A new career?
- Analyst
- Writer or editor
- A solitary position

Hermit combinations

With Hanged Man: Psychic energy; A creative mind holds the power.
With Two of Wands: Starting a new business requires more planning and intense decisions.
With Ten of Cups: The internal search for meaning is a fulfilling endeavor.
Five of Swords: An intense search for a way to win.
With Queen of Pentacles: A person uses her wisdom to gain financial security.

Before any card: Wisdom about (card) is already in your possession
After any card: Knowledge, introspection, solitude

The Major Arcana represent significant, unchangeable life events.
The Hermit could indicate:

- Solitude
- Higher learning
- A literal hermit

X

Wheel of Fortune

The Wheel is the cycle of life - sometimes it
is luck & joy, and sometimes everything
collapses. The baby keeps spinning.

The Wheel of Fortune

The Wheel of Fortune is exactly as it sounds - In most decks it will possess an image of a giant wheel, often with all the symbols of the tarot (and perhaps astrology) inscribed upon it.
It represents the endless cycle of bad luck and good luck that is ever present in our lives.
There is a reason it is one of the middle cards in the Major Arcana, it is a turning point, and continues to turn regardless of what is happening. One moment you are up, and the next moment you are down.

Questions answered by the Wheel of Fortune:

Who? The luckiest or unluckiest person in your family (depending on the subject)
What? Agonize over what you can control, and let the other things go
Where? At the roulette table; wherever you are taking a chance on something
When? November-December; at any time; without warning
Why? Because the cycle of life keeps going, and this is just one part of it
Yes or No? Yes (Reversed: No)

What should I clean?
- The hallway
- The shoe closet

Where are my keys?
- On a circular thing

The Wheel of Fortune as:

An action?
- Take your chances - either you will win, or you will learn

Place in your house?
- Game room or den
- The entryway

Place in your city?
- Wherever you feel lucky
- The casino
- Your boss's office

Place in the world?
- Vegas and Monaco
- Places with intense seasonality, such as the Northeastern US
- Observatories like Mauna Kea

Something to eat?
- Golden fruits
- Tangerines
- Rice
- Cake

A color? White, black

A movie theme? Luck, fortune, cycles of life
- The Lion King
- Yes Man
- Rent

A new career?
- Get in at the very beginning, such as venture capitalism or a startup
- Stock investor
- Pop-up shops and food trucks

The Wheel combinations

With Justice: A conservative person tries not to rock the boat.
With Page of Wands: An exciting new time in one's life.
With Page of Cups: A change in circumstances brings a happy surprise.
Three of Swords: Intense heartbreak is just part of the cycle; recovery is nigh.
With Knight of Pentacles: An unexpected and rapid change in life circumstances.

Before any card: Luck comes in the form of (card)
After any card: Life cycles, luck, the inevitable passage of time

The Major Arcana represent significant, unchangeable life events.
The Wheel of Fortune could indicate:

- A time of good luck
- A time of bad luck
- A year in the life
- A fortuitous event
- A literal wheel

XI

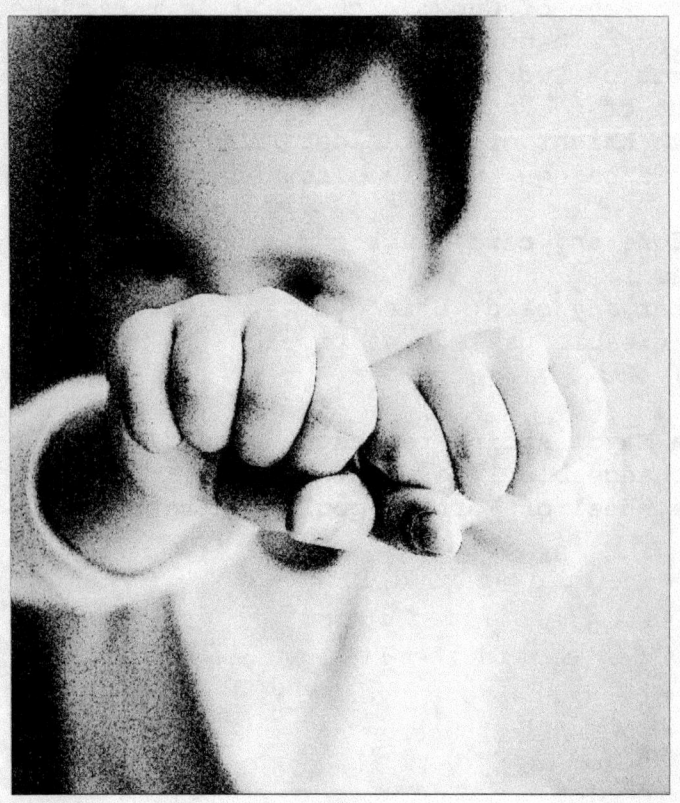

Justice

Justice is cause and effect, law and order, and getting what is deserved. The baby controls the balance of right and wrong.

Justice

Justice is the purveyor of truth and honesty. In almost every deck she bears the scales, weighing right and wrong, and declaring that if you've been good, good things will happen to you. If you have been bad, well - you know.

Usually when Justice is reversed, it is time to pay the price for the wrongs you have committed, but it can sometimes mean that the wrongs that have been committed against you will be rectified.

Questions answered by Justice:

Who? The one who seeks the truth of the matter, such as a judge, parent, or teacher
What? The truth
Where? Somewhere requiring balance, such as the edge of a cliff, your bathroom scale, or on one foot as you put on your shoes
When? When the truth comes out; September-October
Why? Honesty is the best policy
Yes or No? Neutral. The right action will lead to Yes, a dishonest action will lead to No

What should I clean?
- The office
- Pay bills

Where are my keys?
- Under legal paperwork

Justice as:

An action?
- Do a good deed
- Pay your bills

Place in your house?
- The bathroom or kitchen scale (literal)
- The bedroom

Place in your city?
- The courthouse
- A law office or school

Place in the world?
- The Senate of your State or country
- Guantanamo
- Washington, DC

Something to eat?
- A balanced meal
- A healthy breakfast

A color? Grey

A movie theme? Justice, the truth, honesty
- My Cousin Vinny
- The Usual Suspects
- Erin Brockovich

A new career?
- Judge
- Mediator
- Psychotherapist
- Finance
- Historian or Social Studies teacher

Justice combinations

With Chariot: Someone requires permission to do something. Change your password.
With Queen of Wands: Someone is ready to join the effort but needs clarity on that mission first.
With Knight of Cups: A romantic dreamer gets a dose of reality.
With Four of Swords: The truth will be uncovered after a good night's sleep.
With Page of Pentacles: An ambitious and honest young person.

Before any card: The truth comes out about (card)
After any card: Justice, honesty, getting what is deserved

**The Major Arcana represent significant, unchangeable life events.
Justice could indicate:**

- Legal trouble
- Karma catching up to a person
- The truth coming out
- A scale

XII

The Hanged One

The Hanged One is uncertainty & sacrifice, but also patience. The baby surrenders to the events unfolding around them.

The Hanged One

The Hanged One dangles precariously from a tree branch, the vines hung loosely around his or her ankle. But the hanged one is not here against their will - in most decks, you can see the vine knots are tied loosely.

The Hanged One is often in this moment by choice, temporarily sacrificing themself for the greater good.

Questions answered by The Hanged One:

Who? The person who stands to lose the most, but will do so for the greater good
What? A period of transition
Where? Up high, such as in a tree or on a tall shelf; wherever the sacrifices are made.
When? February-March; After a time-out
Why? Because there is an easy way out, you may only need to wait a bit longer to untangle your cords
Yes or No? Maybe. It is situational

What should I clean?
- The fridge
- Dust the door frames and things above you that are not often visible

Where are my keys?
- Where work occurs in the kitchen, such as near the sink, stove, or fridge
- Where you last sat down

The Hanged One as:

An action?
- Sacrifice yourself now for a larger reward later
- Meditate

Place in your house?
- The garden
- The fridge or freezer

Place in your city?
- The park
- A homeless camp
- A nonprofit organization

Place in the world?
- Canada
- A 3rd world country
- HQ of a philanthropy
- Catalonia

Something to eat?
- Fruit
- Vegetables
- Food that others in the household do not want to eat

A color? Turquoise

A movie theme? Sacrifice, patience
- Prison Break
- Interstellar
- Spider-Man: Into the Spider-Verse

A new career?
- Psychology
- Pharmacist
- Artist, Writer, Creative
- Caregiver

Hanged Man combinations

With Wheel of Fortune: A life transition requires a great sacrifice.
With Nine of Cups: Rewards follow hard work.
With Ten of Wands: The sacrifices being made are too much - pare down.
With Four of Pentacles: Someone martyrs themself for financial gain, but it might not be worth it.
With Five of Swords: Much is lost in a fight or battle.

Before any card: A sacrifice must be made for (card)
After any card: Sacrifice, reflection, a momentary pause.

The Major Arcana represent significant, unchangeable life events.
The Hanged One could indicate:

- A sacrifice
- A difficult period of one's life
- A temporary pause
- Something hung

XIII

Death

Death is disruption, chaos, and transformation. The baby weeps at a loss, but transition to a new adventure is imminent.

Death

Death is often the most *feared* card in the tarot deck, but it is definitely not the worst. The death card has the most to teach us about our situation and our life.

In fact, the Death card is more about life and how to live it than other cards in the deck. Death, portrayed typically as the Grim Reaper with a sickle riding a black horse, exists to remind us that the ending of one thing is the beginning of another.

The Death card is like a caterpillar in a cocoon - something we admired may be completely destroyed, but then is reborn even more beautiful.

Questions answered by Death:

Who? The person going through the biggest change or transformation; the Grim Reaper
What? A painful but necessary change
Where? The last place you were when everything changed
When? October-November; stormy weather; quickly
Why? Because you need to let go and trust that the Universe is leading you to something even better
Yes or No? No. Reversed? also no

What should I clean?
- The restroom
- Put out pest control

Where are my keys?
- The tool box
- In the bathroom

Death as:

An action?
- Quit a job
- End a relationship
- Change something
- Move to a new house

Place in your house?
- The closet
- The cat tree
- The medicine cabinet

Place in your city?
- The hospital
- A University
- Court house
- A labyrinth
- A funeral home

Place in the world?
- Bethlehem
- Germany
- A place of great upheaval
- Greece

Something to eat?
- Something new
- Sushi
- Vegan food if you are an omnivore (or vice versa)
- An apple

A color? black

A movie theme? Endings, Transformation
- Up
- Awakenings
- Life is Beautiful

A new career?
- Army
- Funeral work
- Taxes
- Insurance

Death combinations

With Temperance: Someone's patience is wearing thin.
With Knight of Cups: A relationship is ending, or a new one is about to start (depending on the order in which the cards are drawn.)
With Two of Wands: A difficult decision that results in huge change.
With Two of Swords: A total Stalemate. No option is good.
With Ten of Pentacles: A death leads to a large inheritance.

Before any card: A transformation will occur around (card)
After any card: A swift end, a major transformation

The Major Arcana represent significant, unchangeable life events.
Death could indicate:

- A transition
- A transformation
- A brand new career after a job loss
- A new relationship after a divorce
- A death

XIV

Temperance

Temperance is patience, balance, and divine energy. The baby is part of the dynamic flow of water, earth, and heaven.

Temperance

Temperance is commonly confused with Justice, as it does have to do with balance and the scales, however temperance is the emotional side of right and wrong. It is the balance between patience and irritation, between compromise and stubbornness.

Temperance, commonly depicted as an angel pouring equal parts of water between two cups while a volcano explodes in the background, reminds us to stay calm during turmoil in order to get things done. Progress is made when we look at things with a level head.

Questions answered by Temperance:

Who? An energy healer like a Reiki practitioner or a masseuse
What? The moment when things start to come together
Where? In water somewhere, such as a river or sink
When? November to December; When balance occurs; Without notice
Why? Sometimes you must step back to reevaluate the plan
Yes or No? Yes (Reversed: Calm your mind first, then yes)

What should I clean?
- The dishes

Where are my keys?
- Near the sink

Temperance as:

An action?
- Center yourself
- meditate

Place in your house?
- The shower
- A meditation space
- The stove

Place in your city?
- A splash park
- A viewpoint
- A yoga or dance studio

Place in the world?
- The Amazon or Nile
- Mount St. Helens or Pompeii
- The Ancient Roman empire

Something to eat?
- Coffee
- Bananas
- Rice, corn, other grains

A color? Green

A movie theme? Balance, intertwined stories
- Fried Green Tomatoes
- Love, Actually
- Office Space

A new career?
- Mediator
- Humanitarian work
- Travel or foreign diplomacy
- Historian or Anthropologist

Temperance combinations

With High Priestess: Stop and listen to your inner voice.
With Seven of Cups: Daydreaming as meditation.
With Eight of Wands: Travel to a neutral location.
With Six of swords: Have patience with a slower journey.
With Four of Pentacles: Finding balance between frugality and greed.

Before any card: Meditate on (card)
After any card: Moderation, balance, level-headedness

The Major Arcana represent significant, unchangeable life events.
Temperance could indicate:

- A difficult period requiring patience and level-headedness
- A balancing act
- Moderation
- Flooding

XV

The Devil

Devil is attachment, self-victimization, and addiction. The baby is trapped, surrounded by material desires, and unsure of what to do.

The Devil

Looming terrifically over his seemingly helpless victims, the Devil card is another one that evokes fear out of Tarot querants. But in most decks, the devil's victims are there of their own volition, and they have the freedom to leave if they try.

This card is indicative of addictions, greed, and learned helplessness. You *can* break free of your limitations.

Questions answered by The Devil:

Who? The addict, someone who controls you, or yourself when engaging in unhealthy behavior
What? In some way you are deceiving yourself
Where? Wherever you engage in your unhealthiest behaviors
When? December to January; slowly developing over time
Why? Sometimes it's okay to forget about the consequences and take a little break, but be careful not to overdo it
Yes or No? No (Reversed: No, not until you break the chains)

What should I clean?
- The ashtray
- The liquor cabinet
- The unwanted guest's room

Where are my keys?
- Where you last gambled on something
- With your cigarettes or booze

The Devil as:

An action?
- Beat an addiction
- Realize you are jealous, anxious, or delusional, and work on that

Place in your house?
- Wine cellar
- Your wallet
- Where you take your smoke break
- The poker table
- Your bed

Place in your city?
- The casino
- The bar
- The smoke shop

Place in the world?
- Monaco
- An all-inclusive resort
- Las Vegas

Something to eat?
- Fast food
- Shellfish

A color? Brown

A movie theme? Addiction, victimization, torture, attachment
- The Game
- Hellboy
- A Star is Born

A new career?
- Self-employment
- A startup business
- Go back to school
- Mining or other Trades

Devil combinations

With Ace of Wands: Some play is okay right now, just be careful.
With Seven of Cups: A person so addicted to daydreaming that living in reality becomes difficult.
With Magician: A skillful but misunderstood person, perhaps one with a bad reputation.
With Queen of swords: a brilliant but selfish person, or one who is an anachronism.
With Five of Pentacles: Your perceived lack of goods is becoming an addiction. Victim mentality.

Before any card: An addiction to (card)
After any card: Limitations, addictions, restrictions.

The Major Arcana represent significant, unchangeable life events.
The Devil could indicate:

- An addiction
- Imprisonment
- Helplessness
- Fear
- A toxic person in your life

XVI

The Tower

The Tower is sudden upheaval, revelation, or
chaos. The baby's toy verges on disaster.
What is next – trauma, or a fresh start?

The Tower

While the Death and Devil cards tend to scare querants, it is the Tower that is the most overwhelming, as it is more strongly associated with catastrophic ends than Death or Devil. In the Rider-Waite, the image is of a burning building and helpless victims falling to their ultimate demise.

The Tower is a card of sudden and unexpected shock, chaos, and disruption. Will you face the destruction with fear, or with purpose?

Questions answered by The Tower:

Who? The one who controls your fate - such as a boss; Someone who has recently gone through a difficult time
What? Emergency preparations, imminent disaster
Where? A place where disaster has struck
When? March to April, October to November; Immediate and surprising
Why? Tragedy is inevitable
Yes or No? No

What should I clean?
- The worst mess
- The mess you've been trying to avoid

Where are my keys?
- You dropped them somewhere terrible, such as down a grate or into mud

The Tower as:

An action?
- Get your emergency supplies and savings in place

Place in your house?
- The attic
- The phone
- The mailbox

Place in your city?
- The tallest building
- Any place with the name "Tower" in the title
- A school, workplace, or institution with chaotic meaning for you

Place in the world?
- The Burj Khalifa
- Earth's fault lines
- Iraq & Mesopotamia

Something to eat?
- Peppers
- Herbs
- A rare or exotic delicacy

A color? Red

A movie theme? Disaster, chaos
- Titanic
- Jurassic Park

A new career?
- Demolition and construction
- Highly competitive jobs like sales
- The army

Tower combinations

With King of Wands: A leader is prepared for difficult times.
With Four of Cups: Apathy about impending disasters.
With The World: (Tower before) A restart. (Tower after) Total disaster, or the end of the world.
With Nine of Swords: Severe anxiety about a looming disaster - but is it all in your head?
With Six of Pentacles: Helping your community after or before a disaster. Giving back as a way to heal.

Before any card: After a disaster, you will cope best through (card theme)
After any card: A sudden and terrible devastation.

The Major Arcana represent significant, unchangeable life events.
The Tower could indicate:

- Destruction
- Collapse
- A death
- The end of a job or relationship
- A literal tower

The Star

The Star is about hope, healing, and purpose. The baby is content and serene, both on land and at sea.

The Star

After the terror of the Tower comes a card of hope, faith, and inspiration. The Star indicates a blessing from the Universe, one which may not be seen but is felt.

This card typically portrays an individual at peace with themselves, nourishing both the land and the sea, and being creative in their purpose.
In a reading, this card is indicative of renewal and a promising future.

Questions answered by The Star:

Who? Your pet, a therapist, the Dalai Lama, a master of meditation
What? Meditation; the night sky
Where? Somewhere Zen
When? On a clear night; spontaneously; January to February
Why? You are on a healing path, keep it up
Yes or No? Yes

What should I clean?
- The skylights
- The medicine cabinet
- Your mind (meditate)

Where are my keys?
- Somewhere you were in a moment of Zen, unconscious awareness or Highway hypnosis[14]

---

[14] Highway hypnosis occurs when attentions are occupied with things other than the task at hand.

The Star as:

An action?
- Meditate
- Water Plants
- Visualize the future you want

Place in your house?
- The couch
- First aid kit
- The softest carpet

Place in your city?
- Doctor's office
- The hospital
- A serene vista
- A park

Place in the world?
- Nepal
- Mauna Loa observatory
- Stonehenge
- Rio de Janeiro

Something to eat?
- Comfort food
- Food you grew or picked yourself

A color? Blue, white, something shiny

A movie theme? Recovery, healing, stars
- The Shawshank Redemption
- The Pursuit of Happyness
- Independence Day

A new career?
- The entertainment industry
- Public service
- Musician

Star combinations

With Seven of Wands: Do some self-care.
With Ace of Cups: A renewed balance in one's emotions. A calm mind.
With Hierophant: Join a church or a choir, have faith in traditions.
With Four of Swords: It's naptime.
With Ten of Pentacles: Reach out to the family, let them know you are there for them.

Before any card: Have faith in (card)
After any card: Inspiration, hope, creativity

**The Major Arcana represent significant, unchangeable life events.
The Star could indicate:**

- A period of new beginnings
- Hope, inspiration
- The night skies
- Literal stardom

XVIII

The Moon

The Moon is a difficult and dangerous journey. The baby uses imagination and divine messages to push through the dark.

The Moon

The Moon encapsulates the word *foreboding*. It indicates a difficult journey that must be taken in order to move on.

After the Star has rejuvenated and prepared for our fresh Start, the Moon tells us that the path may not be as easy as we expect. It is a card of unconscious darkness - that which we cannot see on the path ahead of us.

Questions answered by The Moon:

Who? The secret keeper; the best liar in the group
What? The Moon; a winding road; a difficult choice
Where? On a hill; downtown at night
When? During a new moon; during a full moon; late June to July; the winter Solstice
Why? Something is being hidden, either by you or from you
Yes or No? Too confusing; currently the answer is no

What should I clean?
- The back of the storage cabinet
- The under-stair storage

Where are my keys?
- Unknown
- Buried and too hidden to see easily

The Moon as:

An action?
- Keep your plan a secret
- A difficult item on your to-do list

Place in your house?
- The window ledge
- A dark space
- The place where the lightbulb needs replaced

Place in your city?
- An observatory
- Twin buildings
- The dog park
- A trail

Place in the world?
- Ecuador
- Area 51
- Bermuda Triangle

Something to eat?
- Turducken
- Melting Chocolate ball

A color? Blue, black

A movie theme? a dangerous journey, mystery
- Back to the Future
- Bird Box
- The Lord of the Rings trilogy

A new career?
- Night watchman
- Detective
- Night work such as lounge singer, sex worker, or third-shift employee

Moon combinations

With Six of Wands: Victory is an illusion.
With Nine of Cups: You are almost ready to go, what item are you forgetting?
With Wheel of Fortune: Everything is cyclical, even this difficult journey.
With Knight of Swords: Someone is delusional.
With Four of Pentacles: Take the difficult path with friends or coworkers.

Before any card: Beware of illusions surrounding (card theme)
After any card: a difficult journey, danger

**The Major Arcana represent significant, unchangeable life events.
The Moon could indicate:**

- Difficult but necessary travel
- Darkness
- Danger
- The literal moon

XIX

The Sun

The Sun is positivity, accomplishment, success, and fun. The baby rests happily in a field of beauty and fortune.

The Sun

The Sun is the happiest card in the deck. Even in a reversed position, the interpretation still promises that the sun will rise again soon. In most decks, the imagery on this card depicts excitement, joy and play.

With this card in a reading, even the most ominous fortunes have positivity and enlightenment in them.

Questions answered by The Sun:

Who? A child at play; the happiest person you know
What? The Sun; flowers; A burst of energy
Where? A sunny location
When? July-August; the summertime; the Summer Solstice; good weather
Why? Because joy is everywhere
Yes or No? YES! (Reversed: also yes, just a bit more subdued)

What should I clean?
- The windows
- Light fixtures

Where are my keys?
- In a sunny spot

The Sun as:

An action?
- It is playtime! Have an adventure

Place in your house?
- A sun-facing window
- The literal sun room
- The playroom

Place in your city?
- The beach
- A lamp store
- A view of the sunset

Place in the world?
- Australia
- The West Coast of America
- Egypt
- The Land of the Midnight Sun (Far North or South, depending on season)

Something to eat?
- Watermelon
- Corn
- Sun-dried tomatoes

A color? Yellow, orange, green

A movie theme? Joy, happiness, fun
- Ferris Bueller's Day Off
- Elf
- Moana

A new career?
- Tutor for young children
- Storyteller
- Amusement park or Cruise Ship operator
- Park ranger or other outdoor job

Sun combinations

With Empress: The mother is happy; the joy of fertility and nature.
With Two of Wands: Find joy in planning.
With Page of Cups: A young, joyful dreamer.
With Nine of Swords: Bipolar disorder; manic depression; the anxiety of finding success.
With King of Pentacles: A successful person who has found abundance.

Before any card: Joyful (card)
After any card: Happiness, joy, a time of great success.

The Major Arcana represent significant, unchangeable life events.
The Sun could indicate:

- The best times
- Happiness
- The literal sun

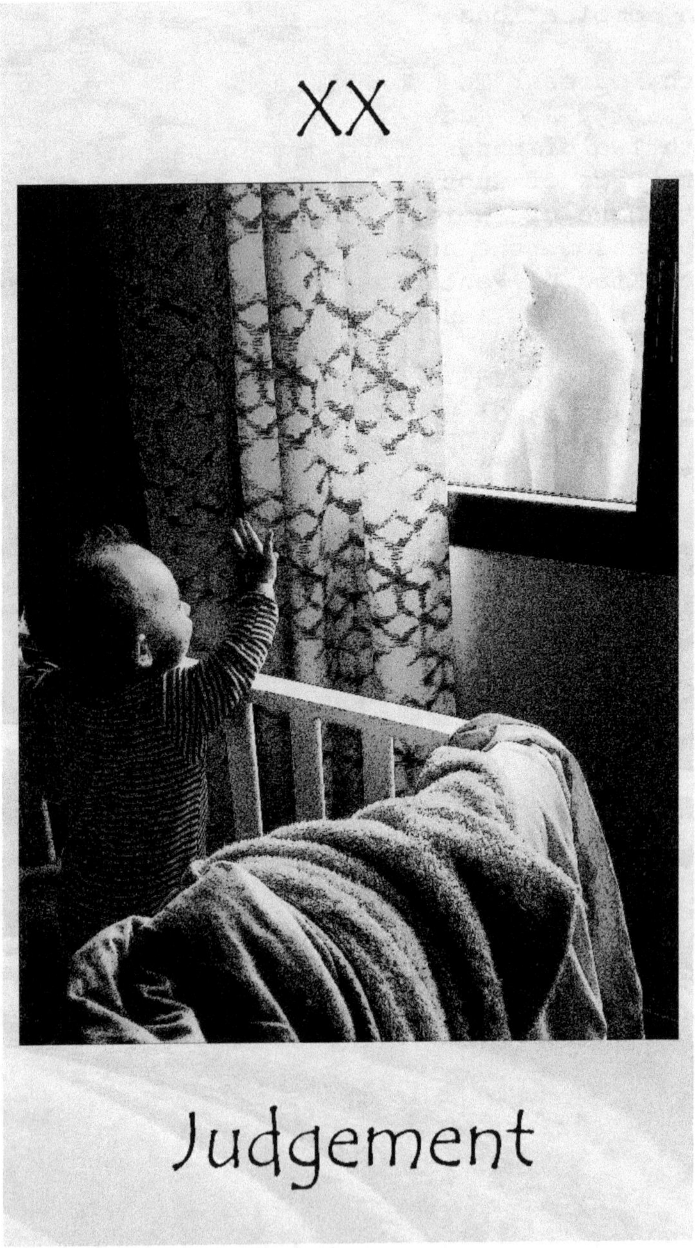

XX

Judgement

Judgement is karma, absolution, and inner calling. The baby calls out to the divine cat for a message about fate and destiny.

Judgement

Judgement is often considered the culmination of your life until this moment, and is seen as positive or negative depending on the karma you have acquired and the choices you have made. Others view it as a destiny card, with other cards showing one's life purpose.

In any reading, it is a lesson that you can change your life by reviewing your past mistakes and making a change for the future.

If things are already good, judgment reminds us that we are never done learning and growing.

Questions answered by Judgement:

Who? The most moral person; a judge
What? A new change based on karma
Where? In the eye of the storm
When? Possibly October-November but no firm astrological dates; During the worst or the best times; Stormy weather
Why? Because eventually karma catches up to you
Yes or No? Have you been good? Then, Yes

What should I clean?
- Your workspace

Where are my keys?
- Wherever the last decision was made

Judgement as:

An action?
- Apologize
- Forgive
- Review the choices you have made
- Revise a plan

Place in your house?
- The basement
- The attic
- The tub or shower

Place in your city?
- The cemetery
- A night club
- A public pool

Place in the world?
- Middle East
- The Mediterranean
- The Iberian Peninsula
- Nepal

Something to eat?
- Vegan diet
- Indian food
- Ethiopian cuisine

A color? Black

A movie theme? Karma, destiny
- Life of Pi
- Almost any origin film in the Marvel Cinematic Universe

A new career?
- Politics
- Human Resources with focus on recruiting or firing
- Career coach or college advisor
- Judge

Judgement combinations

With Hanged Man: Giving too much creates a martyr.
With Three of Wands: The reckoning is coming soon, consider your actions closely.
With Ten of Cups: Dreams come true.
With Two of Swords: Indecision is the undoing. Make a choice now before it is too late.
With Eight of Pentacles: One revisits their successes and failures in order to determine their life's purpose.

Before any card: A reckoning about (card)
After any card: Destiny, fate, absolution

The Major Arcana represent significant, unchangeable life events.
Judgement could indicate:

- One's life purpose
- Karma
- Destiny
- A literal judgement about something

XXI

The World

The World is success, fulfillment, and wholeness. The newborn is a beautiful beginning full of infinite possibility.

The World

The World is the ending and the beginning. The previous card, Judgement, has shown you the lessons from the previous phase of your life, and now it is time to move on to the next amazing step.

Your new "World" might be a graduation, a promotion, an empty nest, a marriage, or any major phase in your life that signifies the end of a chapter and the start of a new one.

Questions answered by The World:

Who? A person going through a significant life change; God
What? Everything; the planet
Where? Everywhere; Where the change happens (or happened)
When? The New Year; Capricorn; Chinese Lunar Year; A slow but intense life change
Why? Because now is the time
Yes or No? Yes (Reversed: yes, but more difficult, and you should question if what you are seeking is worth it)

What should I clean?
- Everything - book a day off and do the whole house

Where are my keys?
- In a place that means the world to you, such as your baby's crib
- On a shelf of heirlooms
- Near the atlas

The World as:

An action?
- Move house
- Change Jobs
- Have a baby
- Try new shampoo

Place in your house?
- The house in its entirety
- Your storage unit

Place in your city?
- The museum
- The city government offices
- A theme park
- Somewhere with "World" in the title, such as *Cartridge World.*

Place in the world?
- The Earth in its entirety
- A place representing the start of a new chapter (of yourself, humanity, etc)

Something to eat?
- Coffee
- Rice
- Noodles or pasta

A color? no color or all colors

A movie theme? Completion, fulfillment
- The original Star Wars trilogy
- Groundhog Day
- Wall-E

A new career?
- A job related to climate awareness
- Natural resources or land use
- Teach overseas
- Government or diplomat jobs

World combinations

With The Devil: The misuse of time; environmental constraints; Limits that are out of one's control.
With Seven of Wands: Maintain control of all that you have achieved.
With Queen of Cups: A gracious and loving, well-traveled older woman.
With Three of Swords: The end of heartbreak. A new beginning.
With Eight of Pentacles: A student of the world; Someone with high standards for success.

Before any card: The successful culmination of (card)
After any card: The world, the best possible outcome

The Major Arcana represent significant, unchangeable life events.
The World could indicate:

- A happy ending
- The culmination of years of hard work
- The literal world

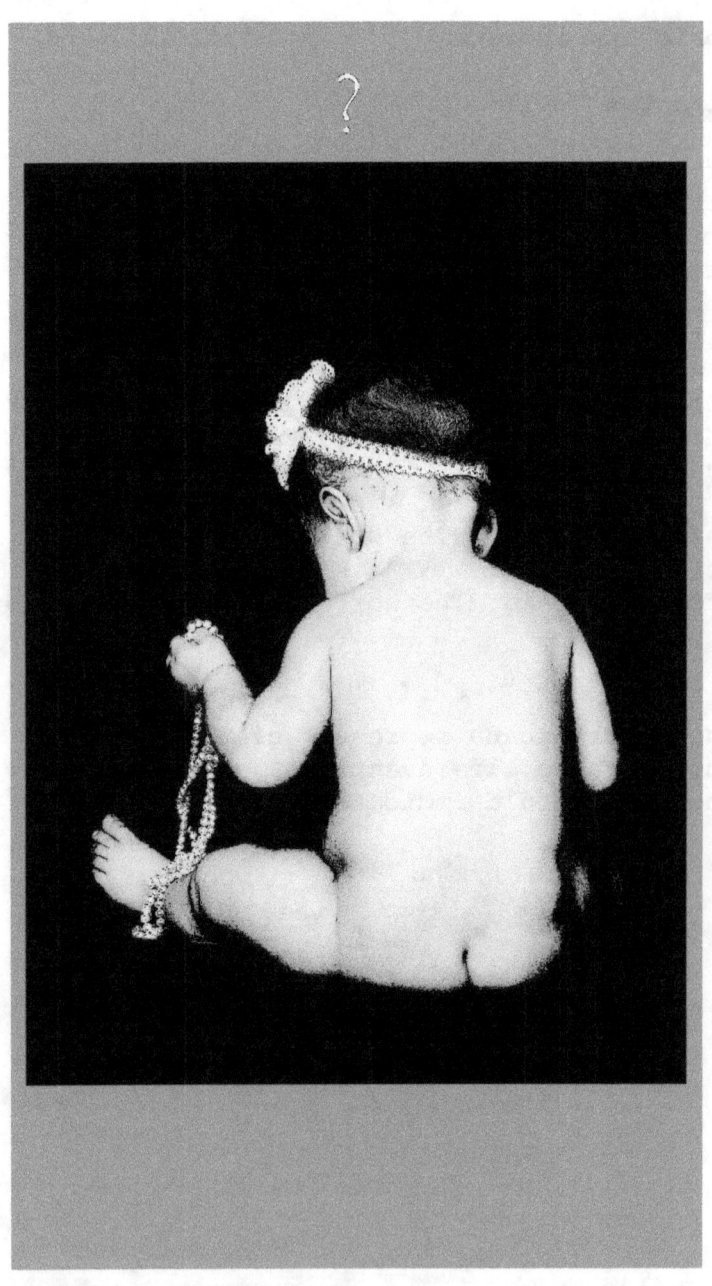

This may be the all-knowing, all-gifted, Millennium, Gratitude, or something else. The baby does not understand the fortune obtained.

The 79th Card

Some Tarot decks have one or more extra Major Arcana cards. Often these can be interpreted as ultimate question cards, the all-knowing or all-gifted, or other specific causes such as Gratitude, Artistry, or Ascension.

For the most part, this card is useless in your quest for simple and practical answers, as it is usually the most powerful, and often asks *you* the question rather than the other way around. But for a general overview of what questions this card may answer, here you go:

Who? Who do you think?
What? What do you think?
Where? Wherever
When? Sometime, or maybe never
Why? Because that's just how life is
How: You figure it out
Yes or No? You tell me

An action? Think about it
Place in your house? Okay
Place in your city? Sure
Place in the world? Yup, that too
Looking for a job? Great! You can do anything!
Food? I'm in!
A color? Whatever you think is best
Movie? Something uncategorizable, such as Eraserhead or Being John Malkovich

What should I clean? You know what you should clean today.

Where are my keys? You will find them when you find them.

79th Card Combinations:

Any combination with this card turns the answer back into a question for your subconscious mind to ponder.
For example, if you asked "what career should I look into" and pulled the Chariot, the 79th card asks you if you like driving a car. Your conscious mind might jump in and say "yes! I love driving!" but ponder it a bit longer and you might realize you'd come to hate driving if you were forced to do it for work.

The 79th card asks you to think and be creative with your ideas.

# The Minor Arcana

What are the Minor Arcana?

The Minor Arcana, also known as the Pips or the Lesser Arcana, are the suit cards. In most decks, they are depicted as wands (or clubs), cups (hearts), swords (spades) and pentacles (diamonds, coins, or disks).

Where the Major Arcana represent huge life-altering events that cannot be radically altered, the Minor Arcana might be people, events, or other everyday goings-on that are mutable and variable. The Minors represent events the querent can affect by changing something about their daily schedule or life.

In general:
- Wands represent air, our instincts, and our career and business.
- Cups represent water, emotions, and our relationships and love life.
- Swords represent fire, knowledge, and the internal conflicts we have in our own minds.
- Pentacles represent earth, money, and the physical and material world that we can see and touch, rather than the instinctual or spiritual world.

The 52 cards of a typical playing card deck can also be used as pip cards, either for divine and nebulous fortune telling, or for the purposes here - simplistic answers to everyday questions.

Sentence Combinations Calculator

I have created this table of words using some of the most rudimentary interpretations from each Minor Arcana card.

In the real world of Tarot, each card would present a variety of meanings based on different contexts, so feel free to replace these words with your own meanings as you see fit.

You can use the following words in any combination and in any structure of phrase. When I ask a question, I typically pick three cards and as each card is drawn, I order them

Verb > Adjective > Noun

Some prepositions you could add between the cards are: about, with, of, at, for, regarding, by, etc.

Wands

	Verb	Adjective	Noun
Ace	Invent	Inspiring	Birth
Two	Plan	Potential	Decisions
Three	Expand	Long-term	Growth
Four	Celebrate	Rewarding	Community
Five	Struggle	Problematic	Competition
Six	Win	Confident	Recognition
Seven	Defend	Persevering	Control
Eight	Hasten	Changing	Movement
Nine	Guard	Resilient	Experience
Ten	Overburden	Laborious	Burden
Page	Energize	Adventurous	News
Knight	Travel	Passionate	Action
Queen	Create	Confident	Joy
King	Influence	Experienced	Leader

Cups

	Verb	Adjective	Noun
Ace	Imagine	Intuitive	Love
Two	Unite	Harmonious	Partnership
Three	Celebrate	Fun	Friends
Four	Contemplate	Indifferent	Apathy
Five	Grieve	Self-pitying	Disappointment
Six	Remember	Caring	Childhood
Seven	Fantasize	Illusory	Daydream
Eight	Retreat	Abandoned	Quest
Nine	Satisfy	Fulfilling	Happiness
Ten	Bless	Peaceful	Fulfillment
Page	Express	Sensitive	Youth
Knight	Flirt	Romantic	Idealism
Queen	Empathize	Loving	Mentor
King	Compose	Calm	Counselor

Swords

	Verb	Adjective	Noun
Ace	Clarify	Intelligent	Truth
Two	Mediate	Impartial	Indecision
Three	Sacrifice	Upsetting	Loss
Four	Restore	Reflective	Rest
Five	Defeat	Irritable	Argument
Six	Journey	Detached	Transition
Seven	Sneak	Deceptive	Strategy
Eight	Imprison	Limiting	Helplessness
Nine	Worry	Scary	Anxiety
Ten	Surrender	Doomed	Closure
Page	Learn	Intellectual	Thinker
Knight	Explore	Revolutionary	Philosophy
Queen	Teach	Self-aware	Communication
King	Assert	Objective	Logic

Pentacles

	Verb	Adjective	Noun
Ace	Invest	Lucky	Opportunity
Two	Juggle	fluctuating	Changes
Three	Contribute	Skilled	Teamwork
Four	Possess	Careful	Resources
Five	Need	Scarce	Poverty
Six	Donate	Giving	Generosity
Seven	Assess	Patient	Evaluation
Eight	Work	Responsible	Task
Nine	Reward	Self-sufficient	Luxury
Ten	Bequeath	Prosperous	Fortune
Page	Study	Skillful	Student
Knight	Honor	Ambitious	Promise
Queen	Protect	Nurturing	Abundance
King	Gain	Reliable	Success

Just now I've asked, "What should I be doing?" and I drew:

King of Pentacles > Nine of Swords > Seven of Pentacles

Using the combinations calculator in Verb/adjective/noun form, I get "gain scary evaluation. I can interpret that to mean "edit your book," because it is a somewhat scary evaluation to analyze and cull one's own work.

I guess I will keep doing that.

A few detailed combinations are included in the card pages. They might expand on these super quick references, or they will show different ways the cards can be interpreted for your situation.

A note on trying to combine the Major Arcana
I do not typically include the Major Arcana in these simple combinations, as there is nothing simple about the Major Arcana - they have a fixed and unwavering meaning and represent a significant moment in your life. The Majors are not good at nitpicking the minutiae of everyday things.

However, do include the Major Arcana if you would like deeper interpretations, or if you do not want to separate them from the deck. If you choose to include them, I recommend you read them as fixed nouns and change your sentence structure accordingly, rather than use them as adjectives and verbs.

The Major Arcana do not describe something else; they *are* the thing you need to know about. Use them as nouns.

The Fool: The Beginning
The Magician: Talent
The High Priestess: Mystery
The Empress: Mother
The Emperor: Father
The Hierophant: Institution
The Lovers: Union
The Chariot: Direction
Strength: Strength
The Hermit: Wisdom
The Wheel of Fortune: Life changes
Justice: Justice
The Hanged Man: Sacrifice
Death: Transformation
Temperance: Balance
The Devil: Entrapment
The Tower: The End
The Star: Hope
The Moon: Risk
The Sun: Joy
Judgement: Judgement, Karma
The World: The World
The 79th card: Questions

So, for example I asked the cards "Why am I struggling to edit today?" and pulled the Page of Wands and The Empress, which is "travel" and "Mother."

I am not surprised at all by this card pull. This week I must book flights for my kids so that they can get back to their respective Universities for the fall semester. However, at the time of writing this book, it is the middle of the Covid-19 pandemic and shutdown, so I am pretty stressed out about their travels, as a Mom.

The Major Arcana are about these unchangeable major events of existence - in my case, my new adult children are moving away to college while the entire world is in a pandemic. There is nothing I can do about any of that, so it is no wonder I am struggling to edit a silly book.

As you draw cards, keep in mind that trying to ask a simple everyday question of the Major Arcana will often get you an answer that is far more overwhelming and unfixable than you might expect.

Now, go forth and...

Queen of Wands   Nine of Cups   Knight of Swords
Verb: Adjective: Noun:
Create   **fulfilling**   **Philosophy**

Or just have some fun with it all!

Wands

Wands represent air, our instincts, or our career and business.

Ace of Wands

Ace of Wands

    The Ace of Wands is the planted seed waiting for water and sun. It is the birth of a new career, a bright idea, or the spark of creativity. It is the moment just before the launch of something new. The Ace of Wands asks the querent to have courage as they set forth into the next phase.
    After the uncontrollable and life-altering Major Arcana cards, this first card in the Minors represents a phase that you yourself *can* control, so go forth and change your world!

The Ace of Wands as:
An action?
- Take a chance
- Leap before you look

Place in your house?
- A room on the top floor that is not a bedroom
- A high shelf

Place in your city?
- The top of your office building
- A viewpoint
- The mountain

Place in the world?
- The World Trade Center
- Big Ben
- Kuala Lumpur
- Beijing

Something to eat?
- Pancakes
- Muesli and Granola bars
- Spring water

A color? Red

A movie theme? Starting brand new
- Kinky Boots
- My Left Foot

A new career?
- Manual or farm labor
- Careers using tools and creative expression

Questions answered by Ace of Wands:

Who? Someone starting a new job; the newest employee; a baby
What? A stick; A pregnancy; A torch
Where? A palace
When? Today! June through September, either the entire season of Summer (Northern Hemisphere) or Winter (Southern Hemisphere)
Why? It is time to take the leap
Yes or No? Yes!

What should I clean?
- An upstairs bathroom
- The laundry

Where are my keys?
- Where you started the last big project

Ace of Wands combinations

With The Sun: There are no negatives here - dive in and whatever you dream, you will achieve.
With Four of Wands: Buy a new home; celebrate at home.
With King of Cups: Start a new job by following your passions.
With Queen of Swords: This next phase is complex, so dive in with a clear and logical mind.
With Nine of Pentacles: Your drive and determination will lead to luxurious rewards.

Before any card: Put emphasis on (card)
After any card: Energy, spirit, goals

Two of Wands

Two of Wands

After the brilliant idea of the Ace, the Two of Wands is going for it!

It is a choice to make and thoughtful planning before you commit. The classic Rider-Waite deck shows a man on the edge of the water, either contemplating his new endeavor, or watching his launched ships as they disappear over the horizon.

After the Ace tells us to launch our new energetic plan, the two is the nerves of it, wondering if everything will work out as we hope.

The Two of Wands as:

An action?
- Write down your plans
- Keep up the momentum

Place in your house?
- The garage
- The new appliance you just purchased
- The front door

Place in your city?
- The highway
- The port or boat launch
- The entrance into town

Place in the world?
- Shanghai
- Porto, Portugal
- Rotterdam
- Delaware

Something to eat?
- Salad
- Lemon, Nanaimo, or Raspberry bars

A color? White, red

A movie theme? Planning
- Ocean's Eleven
- Moneyball

A new career?
- Planning and negotiations
- Leadership and justice

Questions answered by Two of Wands:

Who? Someone puzzling over a problem
What? A globe; A boat; a Project just getting started
Where? Where you go to think about things
When? The last week of March; Aries; within 2 days.
Why? The only way forward is to set one foot in front of the other
Yes or No? An extremely optimistic maybe

What should I clean?
- The kitchen

Where are my keys?
- Where you were last
- The place where you made your last good decision

Two of Wands combinations

With The Moon: The journey ahead is difficult, trust your intuition.
With Ace of Wands: Make a decision, quick!
With Page of Cups: A sensitive person has happy news.
With Ten of Swords: Go ahead but have a plan for failure - We learn the most from our mistakes.
With Eight of Pentacles: If you are contemplating going back to school, do it! (If the eight is reversed, don't do it!) (If the two is reversed, you might not be thinking about school, but you should be!)

Before any card: think about (card)
After any card: Trusting intuition, careful planning.

Three of Wands

Three of Wands

Visually, the Three of Wands often portrays a person on the beach overlooking a fleet of ships. The ships have not quite docked yet, so there is still work to be done. However, this card indicates a time where conditions are favorable for success.
If your plans are in place and you have put the work in, the Three of Wands says your ship will come in!

The Three of Wands as:
An action?
- Take a trip

Place in your house?
- A boat (a picture, a model, or maybe even your boat)
- A place where you can pause to look at your hard work

Place in your city?
- The bridge
- The naval yard or a marina
- A viewpoint

Place in the world?
- The Washington State coast
- Pearl Harbor
- Nova Scotia
- Spain and Portugal

Something to eat?
- A picnic by the water
- Fish and Chips

A color? Red, green, blue

A movie theme? foresight
- Star Trek IV: The Voyage Home
- Dr. Strange

A new career?
- Freelancer
- Inventor
- Global trade

Questions answered by the Three of Wands:

Who? Someone finishing up a project
What? A ship; an overpass; an unfinished project
Where? At the port or marina
When? The first week of April; Within 3 months
Why? Because success is at hand
Yes or No? Yes

What should I clean?
- The laundry
- The Mud room or entryway

Where are my keys?
- Where you finished the last project

Three of Wands combinations

With The Star: Hope is a good thing. "The Secret."[4]
With Ten of Wands: A heavy burden with a great payoff.
With Knight of Cups: Jump in with your whole heart.
With Six of Swords: A difficult transition is necessary for success.
With Seven of Pentacles: The seeds need more time.

Before any card: Watch for (card)
After any card: An event happening soon, the successful completion of a project

---

[4] Byrne, Rhonda (2007) *The Secret.*

Four of Wands

Four of Wands

The Four of Wands is a time of joy, community, and togetherness. After your "ship comes in" with the three, the four represents a chance to celebrate that your hard work has led to success.

You have built a great foundation and a happy home, now it is time to step back and celebrate your efforts with family, friends, and even your dog!

The Four of Wands as:

An action?
- Have a party in your own home

Place in your house?
- Your house itself
- The drawer or cabinet that contains party supplies

Place in your city?
- Your home or neighborhood
- A gathering place for celebrations

Place in the world?
- Your homeland
- Greece
- Israel
- Africa

Something to eat?
- Party food
- Hors d'oeuvres

A color? Red, brown

A movie theme? Community, family
- The Incredibles
- Mamma Mia

A new career?
- Event planner
- Real estate agent
- Designer

Questions answered by the Four of Wands:

Who? Someone at home
What? A house; a gazebo
Where? At home
When? April 11-20; within 4 weeks
Why? Because you deserve a celebration
Yes or No? Yes

What should I clean?
- Do a pass through every room, grabbing one (or four) items of clutter and bring it where it needs to be
- Apply Feng Shui

Where are my keys?
- At home, possibly near your most recently finished project

Four of Wands combinations

With The Tower: Don't fear change, celebrate it.
With Three of Wands: (if 3 precedes 4) Look forward to the day you can celebrate; (If 4 precedes 3) Appreciate your hard work.
With King of Cups: A compassionate older male has reason to celebrate.
With Seven of Swords: You may be celebrating for the wrong reasons - Did you act mischievously to get to where you are?
With Six of Pentacles: Celebrate success but share the wealth with the less fortunate. Not everyone makes it this far.

Before any card: Family togetherness surrounding (card)
After any card: A party, family, a successful meeting

Five of Wands

Five of Wands

When the Five of Wands appears, a conflict has arisen or may happen soon. Perhaps a petty annoyance occurs, or it could be something bigger, like an argument or full on fight.
This card might also represent a sports game or friendly competition.
In the Rider-Waite deck, notice that although the five wand-bearers are scuffling, none are seriously hurt nor extremely angry. It is possible they're in training for an upcoming battle, as well.
The querent should know best what is happening when the Five of Wands pops up.

The Five of Wands as:

An action?
- Do not make a mountain out of a molehill
- Expect a scuffle

Place in your house?
- The gym
- Sports equipment storage

Place in your city?
- The arena
- The gym
- The board game store

Place in the world?
- Turkey
- Athens, Greece
- The location of the next or previous Olympics
- The location of a famous battle

Something to eat?
- Donuts
- Salted meats
- Coffee

A color? Red, blue

A movie theme? competition
- Eurovision Song Contest
- Pitch Perfect
- The Great British Baking Show and other reality competitions (TV)

A new career?
- Sports player or agent
- Talent agent
- Competitive work such as Sales

Questions answered by the Five of Wands:

Who? An athlete
What? A game
Where? At the game
When? July 21-30; within 5 weeks
Why? Because a little competition is good
Yes or No? No. Maybe, if you fight for it

What should I clean?
- Sports or gym equipment
- Mop the floor
- Flip the mattresses

Where are my keys?
- At the gym
- With your sports equipment

Five of Wands combinations

With Death: The end of the fight; "at wit's end."
With Two of Wands: Your perspective is skewed or restricted; Watching the fight.
With Page of Cups: An argument with a sensitive young person.
With Two of Swords: A stalemate, or the inability to reach an agreement.
With Five of Pentacles: Insecurity in battle; The loser of the challenge.

Before any card: A conflict about (card)
After any card: A fight, a game, battle

Six of Wands

Six of Wands

    The Six of Wands is about taking pride in and celebrating one's accomplishments. It could represent *your* win or someone else's. It is a card of pageantry, such as accepting an award, or returning home from a battle to a parade held in one's honor.
    The Six of Wands is the card of victory.

The Six of Wands as:

An action?
- Receive acclaim with grace
- Celebrate the achievements of yourself and others

Place in your house?
- The awards shelf or trophy case
- A video game
- A place you have been celebrated

Place in your city?
- A statue of a famous citizen
- A trophy store
- A location where wins are celebrated such as an arena or parade route

Place in the world?
- Chicago
- Boston
- Ireland
- The UK

Something to eat?
- A hot dog
- A cake
- Food from an award-winning chef or restaurant

A color? Red, brown, green

A movie theme? Victory
- Rocky
- Dead Poet's Society

A new career?
- Work that gets recognition
- Nonprofit Community work

Questions answered by the Six of Wands:

Who? The winner of the game
What? An award show
Where? A trophy shelf or shop
When? First week of August; Six months or years from now
Why? Because you need to celebrate your successes
Yes or No? Yes

What should I clean?
- Your trophies or prizes
- The knife drawer or block

Where are my keys?
- At the last place you celebrated something

Six of Wands combinations

With The Hanged Man: A sacrifice now results in a win.
With Page of Wands: A messenger brings news of a victory.
With Ten of Cups: The prize is inner joy and fulfillment.
With Ace of Swords: A sharp wit is recognized by the public, such as a joke told by a comedian, or an intelligent discussion in a meeting.
With Four of Pentacles: It is time to be humble about your achievements.

Before any card: Successful (card)
After any card: Victory, achievement

Seven of Wands

Seven of Wands

The Seven of Wands is about defending what matters most to you. Typically, the person portrayed in the seven stands alone, fiercely defending his footing against competitors, with no one at his or her side.
Despite the seeming disaster, the shaky footing, and the lone fight, the seven character does have the upper hand, and he or she will not be beaten.

The Seven of Wands as:

An action?
- Stand up for what you believe in
- Join a protest or challenge yourself in something new

Place in your house?
- The front porch
- The attic
- The games room

Place in your city?
- A boxing ring
- A challenging workplace

Place in the world?
- Rome
- Malta
- Finland
- Vietnam

Something to eat?
- Peas and Rice
- Salad
- U-pick, or easy to prepare foods.

A color? blue, brown

A movie theme? perseverance
- The Shape of Water
- Ratatouille

A new career?
- Teacher or Lecturer
- Nonfiction writer
- Defense

Questions answered by the Seven of Wands:

Who? The most defensive person
What? A challenge
Where? A basecamp; one's house
When? The middle of August; Seven units of time from now
Why? Stiff competition is good for you
Yes or No? Yes

What should I clean?
- The fireplace
- The front hall

Where are my keys?
- In a place you need to secure, such as a vault or fine china cabinet
- Inside the front door

Seven of Wands combinations

With Justice: A defense in court.
With Four of Wands: A community protest.
With Nine of Cups: A shopkeeper locks up his wares for the evening.
With Six of Swords: More strategy is needed before proceeding. A debate.
With Ace of Pentacles: Protect something physical, such as a vault or a new car; check your credit report.

Before any card: Maintain control of (card)
After any card: Perseverance, defense

Eight of Wands

Eight of Wands

The Eight of Wands indicates swift energy, action, or travel overseas. The eight wands, typically depicted as flying through the air, indicate that something is coming very soon.

Things are happening rapidly, and you must stay on top of it. Keep your eyes open and your feet ready to go--change is in the air.

The Eight of Wands as:

An action?
- Travel
- Dive in

Place in your house?
- The car
- The travel photo wall

Place in your city?
- The airport
- The train station
- The car dealership

Place in the world?
- The TGV
- Shanghai
- Japan

Something to eat?
- Energy bar
- Airplane food

A color? Blue, green

A movie theme? Travel
- Up in the Air
- Airplane!

A new career?
- Pilot or Flight attendant
- Tourism industry
- Marketing or journalism

Questions answered by the Eight of Wands:

Who? The pilot, driver, or train engineer
What? A trip
Where? The airport
When? The end of November; Very soon; Eight days from now
Why? Change is happening fast
Yes or No? Yes

What should I clean?
- Artwork
- The front porch
- The car

Where are my keys?
- Where your souvenirs are kept
- In the car

Eight of Wands combinations

With Wheel of Fortune: Things are looking up (or down if Wheel is reversed); Be prepared!
With Ace of Wands: Things will happen very soon, possibly in eight minutes or eight hours!
With Eight of Cups: If you have considered walking away from someone or something, do it now!
With Five of Swords: A fight will happen soon.
With Two of Pentacles: A decision must be made quickly.

Before any card: a rapidly approaching (card)
After any card: Travel or swift movement

Nine of Wands

The Nine of Wands is a weary but newly educated person who has endured a great struggle. Many obstacles were overcome, and life is comfortable now, but the querent knows there is always new trouble afoot.

The Nine of Wands calls for inner strength and caution.

The Nine of Wands as:

An action?
- Pull yourself together
- Paint the fence or door
- Check the security system

Place in your house?
- The garden
- The fence or the walls
- A project

Place in your city?
- An old battleground
- The edge of the city

Place in the world?
- Waterloo
- Normandy
- The Aegean Sea
- The place of an ancient great battle

Something to eat?
- Noodles
- Breadsticks

A color? Brown, green

A movie theme? Perseverance
- Backdraft
- 127 Hours
- The Imitation Game

A new career?
- Fitness instructor
- Fireman
- Defense industry work

Questions answered by the Nine of Wands:

Who? The wisest one; the one who has returned from battle
What? A self-fulfilling prophecy
Where? A school or University
When? The first week of December; The future; Nine years from now
Why? You do not always know what to expect, but every challenge is a learning opportunity
Yes or No? Neutral maybe

What should I clean?
- The pantry or food shelves

Where are my keys?
- In the pantry

Nine of Wands combinations

With Hermit: Wisdom gained through purposeful isolation.
With Ten of Wands: Experience leads to a burden of responsibility.
With Seven of Cups: Someone is on a quest for their life's purpose.
With Three of Swords: If we expect the worse, that is what we get.
With Three of Pentacles: The team overcomes obstacles together.

Before any card: be incredibly careful about (card)
After any card: Personal resolve, caution

Ten of Wands

Ten of Wands

The curse wrought by the Ten of Wands is that even when we have succeeded, our work is never finished. This card, typically portraying an exhausted person hauling ten heavy wands, shows us that even when we have earned it all, we need to be vigilant about keeping it.

Sometimes our enthusiasm for a project results in us taking on more responsibility than we can handle.

The Ten of Wands as:

An action?
- Consolidate efforts
- Eliminate clutter

Place in your house?
- The laundry room
- The garage
- Clutter

Place in your city?
- A mall
- The office
- City Hall

Place in the world?
- The Pyramids
- The West coast of USA
- Your country's capital city

Something to eat?
- Peking Duck
- Dumplings
- Pierogis
- A meal that takes a long time to prepare

A movie theme? Burdens
- Bruce Almighty
- Thor: Ragnarok

A new career?
- Many small projects at once
- A brand new career
- A heavy burden

Questions answered by the Ten of Wands:

Who? The most successful but hardest working person
What? A burden
Where? A hotel penthouse; A gym
When? The middle of December; Now; Ten units of time from now
Why? You may be at the risk of physical injury
Yes or No? No

What should I clean?
- The laundry room
- The kitchen
- The messiest room

Where are my keys?
- In the laundry room
- The garage

Ten of Wands combinations

With Strength: A brave person takes on new responsibility.
With King of Wands: Before you take on too much, look at the big picture and prioritize your efforts.
With Six of Cups: The past is a burden; look forward instead.
With Four of Swords: A short break is necessary to restore your energy.
With Page of Pentacles: Ambition is good, but the work may be too great.

Before any card: The burden of (card)
After any card: a heavy workload, a burden

Page of Wands

Page of Wands

The Page of any suit has a lot more freedom than other characters in the Tarot. She, he, or they is young, passionate, engaged and, although intelligent, usually lacks a bit of life experience. Historically, pages were messengers, traveling around the kingdom to bring news between the royals. Tarot pages are these messengers.

When you see the Page of Wands, expect news regarding something creative, innovative, or entrepreneurial.

The Page of Wands as:

An action?
- Write down your 6-month, 1 year, and 5-year goals
- Start that new project

Place in your house?
- The mailbox
- The baby's room

Place in your city?
- A startup incubator
- An art house

Place in the world?
- San Francisco
- Toronto
- Germany
- Shanghai

Something to eat?
- An orange
- Fresh picked fruit
- Lamb

A color? Red, orange, yellow, brown

A movie theme? New adventures
- Jumanji
- Spider-Man: Homecoming

A new career?
- Working with children
- Activism
- Creative nonprofit work

Questions answered by the Page of Wands:

Who? A young storyteller
What? A message about something new
Where? A place of creative energy
When? Summertime (Northern Hemisphere) or Winter (Southern Hemisphere); When the next new thing begins
Why? It is time to start a new project!
Yes or No? Yes!

What should I clean?
- The baby's room
- The play room

Where are my keys?
- In the crafts closet
- In the baby's room

Page of Wands combinations

With Chariot: A road trip to somewhere you have never been.
With Seven of Wands: Defend your choice, maintain control of your emotions, and keep moving toward your destiny; Leave the naysayers behind.
With Five of Cups: A new endeavor may not work out exactly as planned, but there is hope ahead; stay focused.
With Two of Swords: A difficult choice must be made about a project.
With Ace of Pentacles: A message arrives about a new opportunity.

Before any card: Someone brings an inspiring message about (card)
After any card: Something new and creative

Knight of Wands

Knight of Wands

    The Knight of Wands charges into the scene, taking bold risks with passion and fun. This knight also has a short attention span and does not stay in one place for long. While the knight can quickly change direction when things are not working out, they may also grow bored of jobs, relationships, or other things that are otherwise healthy.
    This knight often values new adventure over common sense.

The Knight of Wands as:

An action?
- Travel somewhere new

Place in your house?
- The games room
- Where the shoes are stored

Place in your city?
- An indoor racing center
- The skate park
- Horse riding

Place in the world?
- Indianapolis Motor Speedway
- France
- Pamplona

Something to eat?
- Tea
- Cherries
- Whole grains
- A protein bar

A movie theme? adventure, risk-taking
- Finding Nemo/Finding Dory
- Die Hard

A new career?
- Jobs involving fast driving such as EMT or Pilot
- Competitive work such as sales

Questions answered by the Knight of Wands:

Who? A person who cannot stay in one place for long; An equestrian
What? A new challenge
Where? The races
When? Mid July to mid August; A short amount of time
Why? Because adventure awaits!
Yes or No? Yes

What should I clean?
- Hall closet or shoes
- Trunk of the car
- Travel gear such as camping supplies

Where are my keys?
- In your shoes
- Near the front door
- In the car

Knight of Wands combinations

With Lovers: One is stronger with a partner.
With Six of Wands: Taking bold action leads to victory.
With Four of Cups: Someone questions their purpose. A moment of reflection may be needed before diving in.
With King of Swords: One discovers the truth about themself - they must be bold but disciplined.
With Two of Pentacles: Prioritize the options before jumping in.

Before any card: An energetic person brings an item related to (card)
After any card: Swift movement, a bold risk.

Queen of Wands

Queen of Wands

The Queen of Wands is independent, confident, and beautiful. Sitting atop a sunny throne, the Queen looks off into the distance to keep an eye on everything in their command.

The queen represents extroversion and friendliness, while still being self-reliant and self-contained. The Queen has done it all by the Queen's self, and success shows.

The Queen of Wands as:

An action?
- Make a list of all your successes
- Be confident and go forth into new projects

Place in your house?
- The family room
- The rocking chair

Place in your city?
- A woman-owned business
- A geriatric care center
- A school

Place in the world?
- Indonesia
- Israel
- Ghana
- Russia
- One's birthplace

Something to eat?
- Sunflower seeds
- Pasta or noodles
- Fruits

A color? Yellow, red, orange, brown

A movie theme? Creativity
- Exit Through the Gift shop
- Frida

A new career?
- Teacher
- Entrepreneur

Questions answered by the Queen of Wands:

Who? A female-presenting boss; The Queen; a mother figure
What? A passion project or hobby
Where? A woman-owned business
When? March and April; Enough time to mature
Why? Because the best time to start something was 10 years ago, the second-best time is now
Yes or No? Yes

What should I clean?
- The home office

Where are my keys?
- Where women rule

Queen of Wands combinations

With Hierophant: One puts their own creative spin on a steadfast tradition.
With Five of Wands: Competition is fierce, but the courage and determination will lead to victory.
With Three of Cups: One is even more successful with friends on their side.
With Knight of Swords: Jump in!
With Ten of Pentacles: A powerful woman leaves a legacy to family or employees.

Before any card: a passionate person/woman starts a project involving (card)
After any card: Confidence, business success

King of Wands

King of Wands

    The King of Wands is a powerful and commanding community leader, such as a political figure or CEO. The King is devoted and loyal to family, friends, and employees, but sometimes the King's competitive nature can get the best of them - tempers may flare or a gamble taken may be too big.
    In the end, the King carries on with optimism no matter what.

The King of Wands as:

An action?
- Start a new, challenging project
- Take a risk on something

Place in your house?
- The office
- The sofa
- A place where Dad sits

Place in your city?
- A large organization
- The legislature

Place in the world?
- Greece
- Portugal
- The Middle East

Something to eat?
- Asian fusion or other cuisines blended from multiple regions
- Tacos

A color? Red, green, brown, orange, yellow

A movie theme? Influential leadership
- Black Panther
- Schindler's List

A new career?
- Boss
- Politics
- Finance

Questions answered by the King of Wands:

Who? A CEO; A King; A father figure
What? A financial gain
Where? A law office
When? August or November; a few years
Why? Being honest is the way to success
Yes or No? Yes

What should I clean?
- Paper clutter related to work or financial issues

Where are my keys?
- Under a pile of paperwork

King of Wands combinations

With Empress: A baby is coming, or a family is in the big picture.
With Three of Wands: Work hard and keep your eyes on the prize.
With Two of Cups: Forming a partnership results in success (starting business in the US? Do an LLC vs. sole proprietorship)
With Ten of Swords: A bold risk fails. Be confident but extra cautious.
With Four of Pentacles: "Praise Allah, but first tie your camel to a post.[5]" meaning go ahead and take a leap, but first make sure you have the basics figured out.

Before any card: A person/man teaches about or shows you something involving (card)
After any card: A new job or opportunity

---

[5] Attributed to the Prophet Mohammed

Cups

Cups represent water, emotions, and our relationships and love life.

Ace of Cups

The Ace of Cups is the beginning of one's social or emotional journey. A giant hand reaches out from the clouds, holding a cup that runneth over, indicating that the querant is surrounded by copious amounts of love, joy, and happiness.

When the Ace of Cups appears, trust your emotional value, and open yourself to messages from the Universe.

The Ace of Cups as:

An action?
- Road trip with friends
- Romantic getaway with a partner
- Allow your feelings to flow

Place in your house?
- The bathtub
- The bar
- The dining room table

Place in your city?
- A park fountain

Place in the world?
- A coastal city
- Hawai'i
- Quebec
- Denmark
- South Africa

Something to eat?
- Tiramisu
- Yogurt and Granola
- Cocktails

A color? Blue, yellow, white

A movie theme? New passion
- Under the Tuscan Sun
- 20 Feet from Stardom
- Happy Gilmore

A new career?
- Hospitality
- Creative work
- Beauty industry
- Yoga or meditation

Questions answered by Ace of Cups:

Who? Someone who has just fallen in love; a new friend
What? A cup; A bottle of wine
Where? At a waterfall
When? Now; The entire season of Fall (Northern Hemisphere) or Spring (Southern Hemisphere)
Why? Make a fresh start in romance or friendship
Yes or No? Yes

What should I clean?
- The shower or bathtub
- The sink
- The glasses

Where are my keys?
- Near water

Ace of Cups combinations

With Emperor: A Dad's heart melts; an authority figure softens their mood.
With Two of Wands: Listen closely to your intuition.
With Seven of Cups: A daydream about love.
With Page of Swords: A young, passionate person brings important news.
With Queen of Pentacles: Someone is pregnant or is a new Mom.

Before any card: A divinely inspired (card)
After any card: Emotional fulfillment.

Two of Cups

Two of Cups

The Two of Cups is the real Lovers card. While the Major Arcana Lovers represents more of a melding of the head and the heart, the Two of Cups is true companionship. It is the Yin and Yang.

The couple represented by the two are nothing without each other, and the blending of their two hearts will lead to success in relationship, companionship, business, or friendship.

The Two of Cups as:

An action?
- Form a partnership
- Contact your partner

Place in your house?
- A bed
- A loveseat
- A place with items in pairs.
- The back-right corner of your house (Feng Shui)

Place in your city?
- A romantic restaurant
- A business run by two partners
- A park

Place in the world?
- Paris
- Virginia
- Goa
- Italy
- Brazil

Something to eat?
- Chocolate strawberries
- Oysters

A color? blue, red

A movie theme? True love, partnership
- Romeo + Juliet
- Once
- 50 First Dates

A new career?
- Marriage therapist
- Officiant
- Healer or caretaker

Questions answered by Two of Cups:

Who? A lover, a best friend, or a business partner
What? A date, or a meeting of two minds
Where? A romantic location
When? The last week of June; 2 units of time.
Why? Equality and respect is key
Yes or No? Yes

What should I clean?
- Make the bed

Where are my keys?
- In the bed
- The last place you were with another person

Two of Cups combinations

With High Priestess: A meeting of the minds.
With Page of Wands: An exciting new partnership, possibly with a younger person.
With Six of Cups: Happy memories about family and love; Possibly a pregnancy on the horizon.
With Nine of Swords: Mutual anxiety; Trauma about a partnership or relationship
With Knight of Pentacles: Everyone must put equal amounts of hard work into the business to keep it going.

Before any card: Harmony within (card)
After any card: Partnership or relationship

Three of Cups

Three of Cups

Where the two is about romantic love or a bonding partnership, the three is about platonic love, community, and friendship.

The immense joy and the feeling of togetherness is at the same scale in both cards. Where the two is about a couple or two people, the three is about the entire team, or a group of friends who love and need each other.

The Three of Cups as:

An action?
- Reach out to friends
- Throw a party

Place in your house?
- The back patio
- The garden
- A game room
- Kitchen or bar

Place in your city?
- A club
- A casual restaurant
- A volleyball court

Place in the world?
- New York City
- Portland
- Ireland
- Mexico

Something to eat?
- Party sub
- Pizza
- Wine
- Chips and dip

A color? yellow, orange, red

A movie theme? Friendship
- A League of Their Own
- Bridesmaids
- The Hangover
- 9 to 5

A new career?
- Event planner
- Social worker
- Hospitality
- Creative collaboration

Questions answered by Three of Cups:

Who? A group of friends; The team
What? A toast; A party
Where? A hangout spot
When? The first week in July; 3 months.
Why? There is always time for friends.
Yes or No? Yes

What should I clean?
- The wine glasses
- The cabinet with mugs

Where are my keys?
- Under the sofa
- On the dining room table

Three of Cups combinations

With Magician: A group of friends create magic together.
With Queen of Wands: An older, wiser female-presenting individual becomes a great companion and resource.
With Five of Cups: The potential loss of a friendship unless something is fixed soon.
With Eight of Swords: You may feel trapped or stifled by your friends, but you have the power to break free of them and choose your own path.
With Page of Pentacles: A message from a friend arrives.

Before any card: A collaborative (card)
After any card: Friendship or community

Four of Cups

Four of Cups

    Fours are stable cards. The best way to describe fours is to picture them as the four corners of a table. Three legs and it may topple, five legs is superfluous, but four is a solid base.
    However, with the stability of the number four comes a bit of boredom and apathy, too. The four of cups *is* that apathy, when we tell ourselves "Everything is fine, so why bother?"
    In common depictions of this card, a person sits alone, indifferent to the cup of joy being directly handed to them. It is boring.

The Four of Cups as:

An action?
- Daydream, but keep your eyes open for reality's gifts
- Meditate

Place in your house?
- A lounge chair
- The sofa

Place in your city?
- The lawn at a park
- A comfy place to sit
- A large tree

Place in the world?
- Ottawa, Canada
- Oslo, Norway
- Wellington, NZ
- Zurich, Switzerland

Something to eat?
- Air-popped popcorn
- Beef jerky
- Crudités
- Rice cakes with peanut butter

A color? Green

A movie theme? Apathy
- The Big Lebowski
- Lost in Translation

A new career?
- Executive or Administrative assistant
- Code monkey
- Someone in the background

Questions answered by Four of Cups:

Who? Someone with a boring job, such as an accountant or security guard
What? A dull moment
Where? Under a tree; right in front of you
When? The middle of July; 4 months; When you stop daydreaming and start doing.
Why? Opportunities are available if you look up
Yes or No? Meh

What should I clean?
- A pile of clutter that has been sitting around awhile

Where are my keys?
Where you last sat or laid down

Four of Cups combinations

With Fool: After a moment of contemplation, inspiration will strike.
With King of Wands: A powerful leader needs a minute to disconnect.
With Ace of Cups: Boredom is a great time to listen to your intuition; meditate.
With Seven of Swords: Someone is using "I need Downtime" as an excuse to be lazy.
With Ten of Pentacles: The kids are watching - be careful not to complain about how boring life is. You may create a legacy of apathetic persons.

Before any card: Boredom toward (card)
After any card: Indifference or Apathy

Five of Cups

Five of Cups

If we imagine pulling cup cards in succession, it is highly likely that the laziness we felt during the four of cups turned into a deep regret about our inactivity.

That's the five of cups. It is the regret or grief about something that happened in the past. However, it also reminds us to look for the good. In classic decks, a forlorn person stares at three overturned cups, but he need only to turn around and see that two still remain upright.

The five of cups is an instruction to lift your chin up and look around you, there may be no need for this much despair.

The Five of Cups as:

An action?
- Look for the good
- Start a gratitude journal
- Change something

Place in your house?
- The mantel
- The photos

Place in your city?
- The river
- A bridge
- Your favorite restaurant needs your business

Place in the world?
- Germany
- Japan
- Indonesia

Something to eat?
- Ice Cream
- Nuts

A color? black, grey

A movie theme? disappointment
- Inside Out
- Marriage Story
- The Fifth Element

A new career?
- Isolating hospitality work, such as a closing bartender, hotel auditor, or night nurse
- Counselor

Questions answered by Five of Cups:

Who? Someone with a lot of regret.
What? Disappointment
Where? Behind you
When? The last week of October; 5 years ago; 5 units of time from now
Why? with loss comes change
Yes or No? No

What should I clean?
- The area behind you

Where are my keys?
- Where you made your last mistake

Five of Cups combinations

With Magician: A miserable person does not realize they have the tools needed to recover.
With Knight of Wands: (before 5) a bold and fearless person dives into something they later regret, or (after 5) a sad person takes a chance on a new adventure.
With Two of Cups: Two people are feeling a loss. (2 before 5) Going through a divorce, or (5 before 2) Divorce brings you closer to your ex - you are better as friends.
With Six of Swords: The transition through grief is a terrible journey, but the right one. A journey is difficult but short.
With Nine of Pentacles: You've done things you regret to make it to the top. It is time to look back and repair the damage.

Before any card: Disappointment in (card)
After any card: Grief, regret, sadness

Six of Cups

Six of Cups

In its simplest form, the Six of Cups is about childhood. It could mean literal children or might represent a nostalgia for those moments where we were at our most innocent.

Take a deeper look at the meaning, and you may find you are stuck in the past or clinging to memories that are no longer realistic. The children depicted in the Six represent a type of love that adults find hard to obtain - that of innocence and purity.

The Six of Cups as:

An action?
- Play
- Don't linger on what was, focus on what is
- Hang out with the kids

Place in your house?
- A child's bedroom
- The playroom

Place in your city?
- A play park
- An amusement park
- A primary school

Place in the world?
- Disney
- An amusement park
- Toronto
- San Diego

Something to eat?
- Dino nuggets
- Grab and go snacks
- A happy meal
- A banana

A color? yellow, red

A movie theme? childhood, nostalgia
- Hot Tub Time Machine
- Pleasantville
- The LEGO movie

A new career?
- Working with children
- Forensic investigator or historian

Questions answered by Six of Cups:

Who? A child
What? A toy
Where? In a child's space
When? The first week of November; In the distant past; When a child is a little older
Why? The past is the past
Yes or No? Yes

What should I clean?
- The child's bedroom
- The playroom

Where are my keys?
- Your kid or dog probably took them

Six of Cups combinations

With High Priestess: Trust your inner child - what would you have done way back then?
With Seven of Wands: Something related to children has you on the defensive. Find a way to persevere without compromising your values.
With Four of Cups: You are wallowing about something in the past.
With Five of Swords: You may be fighting a losing battle - Are you repeating past mistakes?
With King of Pentacles: A successful matriarch or patriarch leaves a legacy to many children.

Before any card: Nostalgia or memories about (card)
After any card: childhood, memories

Seven of Cups

Seven of Cups

Seven of Cups is the fantasy, the daydream. For some tarot readers, it represents a drug-induced trip; For others, it is a set of options to choose from.
A precise interpretation of the Seven may be less important than how the querent themself imagines the meaning to be. Is it a fantasy? A dream? An actual choice between a disembodied head and a laurel wreath (two of the cards depicted in the Rider-Waite?) Or is it something that is completely unknowable to you at this time?

The Seven of Cups as:

An action?
- First dream wildly, then act
- Have a lucid dream

Place in your house?
- A good place to nap
- A meditation room
- The shower

Place in your city?
- A fancy hotel
- A museum
- A gallery

Place in the world?
- Disney
- New York City
- Tokyo
- Iceland
- The Mediterranean

Something to eat?
- Late night snacks
- Water
- Candy

A color? blue

A movie theme? fantasy, dreaming
- Inception
- The Secret Life of Walter Mitty
- Alice's Adventures in Wonderland

A new career?
- Career or educational advisor
- Handyman
- Ideas person
- Nonprofit work

Questions answered by Seven of Cups:

Who? The dreamer
What? A dream
Where? In a fantasy world; in a place you can picture but cannot touch - yet
When? The middle of November; In your dreams; Seven hours or days from now (A short amount of time)
Why? "The biggest adventure you can take is to live the life of your dreams"[6]
Yes or No? Probably not

What should I clean?
- The bedroom

Where are my keys?
- Your bed or the last place you napped.

Seven of Cups combinations

With Empress: The dream of having a baby; A baby sleeps; The Natural world.
With Four of Wands: Someone searches for a new home or community.
With Three of Cups: A dream about a friend; Hoping for the best for a loved one.
With Three of Swords: Too much fantasy leads to heartbreak in the real world. (If the 3 leads, a dream of a better tomorrow.)
With Eight of Pentacles: A student imagines his life after graduation; A dream of going back to school.

Before any card: A fantasy about (card)
After any card: fantasies, daydreams

---

[6] Oprah Winfrey

Eight of Cups

Eight of Cups

    The Eight of Cups is another card which has different meanings based on context. The eight typically portrays a person quietly walking away from his or her stash of cups. Are they going on a spirit quest? Are they disappointed with their cups and looking for something else, or are they desperate for more? Are they disillusioned with the present and ready to move on to the future, or are they just in need of a short break?
    This Eight is best interpreted in the moment.

The Eight of Cups as:

An action?
- Move to a different location
- Start something different
- Look for a better solution

Place in your house?
- A room or space you don't visit often

Place in your city?
- A new house or job
- An open house
- A hiking trail

Place in the world?
- The wilderness
- India
- Nepal
- The Alps

Something to eat?
- Trail mix
- A platter of random items
- Leftovers

A color? blue

A movie theme? abandonment, retreat
- The Secret of NIMH
- Good Will Hunting

A new career?
- Something completely different
- Spiritual work
- Retire

Questions answered by Eight of Cups:

Who? A seeker
What? A hike
Where? Not here
When? The end of February; 8 days; When you get back from your trip
Why? We all need time alone to contemplate our emotions
Yes or No? No

What should I clean?
- A room you do not visit often

Where are my keys?
- Where you last put a bunch of things down.
- You keep walking right by them

Eight of Cups combinations

With Emperor: Don't trust the patriarchy, seek out a new authority.
With Ace of Wands: Someone becomes disillusioned with a project.
With Queen of Cups: Despite an abundance of empathy and compassion for someone, it is still time to move on from them.
With King of Swords: Trust your logical mind in your decision to leave; Walking away from an authority.
With Seven of Pentacles: It will take perseverance to walk away and plant new seeds elsewhere.

Before any card: Walk away from (card)
After any card: Abandonment, escape

Nine of Cups

Nine of Cups

The Nine of Cups is riches and luxury. The card typically shows a person, perhaps a shopkeeper, happily surrounded by their wares and proud to show them off.

Because cups are about emotion, this card represents the feelings involved when you are surrounded by your goods or possessions. It is satisfaction, appreciation, and pleasure, and sometimes a bit of smugness too.

Go ahead and open your store for sale, you are ready.

The Nine of Cups as:

An action?
- Enjoy a piece of art
- Show gratitude
- Visualize success
- Open your shop

Place in your house?
- An art piece, or a shelf with your prized possessions

Place in your city?
- A gallery or museum
- The bank that holds your money
- A Mom & Pop shop

Place in the world?
- The Vatican
- New York
- Pike Place Market, Seattle
- Grand Bazaar, Turkey
- Morocco
- Singapore

Something to eat?
- Doner kebab
- Tacos
- Tagine
- Curry

A color? Yellow

A movie theme? wish fulfillment
- Aladdin
- The Great Gatsby
- Willy Wonka and the Chocolate Factory

A new career?
- Shopkeeper
- Mentor
- Luxury goods
- Homemaker
- Retiree

Questions answered by Nine of Cups:

Who? A contented wealthy person
What? items of value
Where? A comfy chair
When? The first week of March; 9 months
Why? It's okay to celebrate your blessings
Yes or No? Yes

What should I clean?
- Dust the knick-knack shelves
- Do the dishes

Where are my keys?
- Near your prized possessions

Nine of Cups combinations

With Hierophant: Following established traditions brings great fulfillment.
With Ten of Wands: Heavy burdens result in riches
With King of Cups: A mature wealthy person shares wealth with the underprivileged
With Four of Swords: When you have achieved satisfaction, it is time to take a break.
With Six of Pentacles: As you give unto others, you will be blessed in kind.

Before any card: Showcase and be proud of (card)
After any card: The attainment of luxury, success

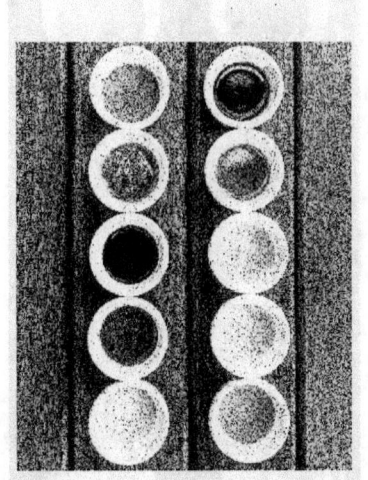

Ten of Cups

 The Ten of Cups is the ultimate emotional fulfillment card. A happy family is indicated in almost any deck. The Ten is not about immense wealth or luxury--although that could certainly be indicated by other cards in a spread--but instead, it is about obtaining the highest level of gratitude and emotional abundance.
 Seeing the Ten of Cups in any reading is a great blessing. Even reversed, the emotional fulfillment may be lacking, but there is lots to be grateful for if you look around.

The Ten of Cups as:

An action?
- Be grateful for your blessings
- Start a gratitude journal
- Spend time with your family

Place in your house?
- Where your loved ones spend the most time
- The dining table.

Place in your city?
- A church
- The community center
- The park
- A mall

Place in the world?
- Denmark
- Iceland
- New Zealand
- Disney parks

Something to eat?
- Casserole
- Pasta
- A recipe passed down from an ancestor

A color? Happiness, family
- 10 Things I Hate About You
- The Addams Family
- Coco

A new career?
- Publicity
- Fame
- Sales
- Creative arts

Questions answered by Ten of Cups:

Who? The happiest person; the family
What? Sheer joy
Where? A playground
When? The middle of March; 10 years;
Why? "Family is not an important thing. It's everything.[7]"
Yes or No? Yes

What should I clean?
- The dining room table
- The Kitchen

Where are my keys?
- A loved one has them
- A child ran away with them during play

Ten of Cups combinations

With Lovers: Committing to a partnership leads to a lifetime of fulfillment
With Nine of Wands: Having gratitude requires work - Write down things you are grateful for.
With Knight of Cups: Trust your heart over your head and wishes will be fulfilled.
With Three of Swords: There is love in heartbreak. Ever mind the rule of three, what ye send out comes back to thee[8]
With Five of Pentacles: Focusing on wants not haves. Without love there is poverty.

Before any card: Be grateful for (card)
After any card: Blessings, success, family

---

[7] Michael J. Fox
[8] Universal prophecy commonly attributed to Wiccan or Pagan rituals

Page of Cups

Page of Cups

    The Page of Cups typically portrays a young romantic offering up a cup with the gift of a fish. One might imagine they are handing it to their new love or crush.
    This young person is creative and kind, possibly an artist or musician on the side, while they figure out what they want to learn next.
    This Page wants to be helpful but is a little shy about asking what you need from them.

The Page of Cups as:

An action?
- Help someone
- Go fishing
- Love yourself
- Give a gift

Place in your house?
- The bathroom
- A child's room
- A pond in the garden

Place in your city?
- A water or play park
- A romantic restaurant
- A seafood restaurant.

Place in the world?
- Australia
- PEI or Northern Canada
- Mexico
- A great fishing spot

Something to eat?
- Seafood you caught yourself
- Chowder
- Fish

A color? blue, pink

A movie theme? Cautious new love
- Notting Hill
- Amélie
- Sky High

A new career?
- Poet, Artist, Musician, or other Creative
- Youth worker
- Veterinarian or animal worker
- Fishing or working with fish

Questions answered by Page of Cups:

Who? A romantic
What? A cup of soup
Where? A water park
When? Autumn (Northern Hemisphere); Spring (Southern Hemisphere); At first sight; Very soon
Why? "You can't use up creativity. The more you use, the more you have"[9]
Yes or No? Yes

What should I clean?
- The bathroom

Where are my keys?
- In the kitchen or bathroom
- Near a cup or mug you are using

Page of Cups combinations

With Chariot: Move swiftly in the direction of your heart's desire.
With Eight of Wands: Love arrives swiftly, as in love at first sight. One travels to see their partner.
With Three of Cups: Being with friends brings joy.
With Ace of Swords: A quick-witted, logical conversation with a young, creative person.
With Queen of Pentacles: A new baby; a pregnancy; a loving mother.

Before any card: Passion or creativity involved with (card)
After any card: Young person, creativity

---

[9] Maya Angelou

Knight of Cups

The Knight of Cups rides passionately into love and romance. Where the Page is more timid, the knight is confident in his drive and creativity. He is willing to jump into new and exciting adventures that might bring him more risk but could also lead to greater reward.
The message from this knight is follow your heart, quick!

The Knight of Cups as:

An action?
- Chase a dream
- Ask a psychic about your purpose
- Buy some new art pieces

Place in your house?
- An art piece
- A place of romance
- The couple's bed

Place in your city?
- A home decor store
- An art shop
- A theatre

Place in the world?
- The Poconos
- Yellowstone
- Amsterdam
- The Caribbean

Something to eat?
- Fish you caught yourself
- Oysters
- Salmon

A color? blue, grey

A movie theme? Emotional intensity
- Brokeback Mountain
- La La Land
- The Notebook

A new career?
- Artist
- Composer
- Theatre Director
- Romance Novelist
- EMT

Questions answered by Knight of Cups:

Who? The one who takes the most risks with his or her heart
What? A goal or dream
Where? A river
When? Mid-October to Mid-November; relatively soon
Why? Feelings can change quickly
Yes or No? Yes

What should I clean?
- The laundry
- The freezer or fridge

Where are my keys?
- Near something artistic
- Your lover has them

Knight of Cups combinations

With Strength: Have confidence as you dive in - this is right!
With Six of Wands: An endeavor is successful; a whirlwind romance leads to a celebration.
With Five of Cups: Diving in too fast leads to some regretful mistakes. Think all possibilities through first.
With Queen of Swords: A man falls in love with a complex woman; Someone is very direct with their romantic partner.
With Four of Pentacles: Marriage brings security, protection, and equal love to all partners.

Before any card: A romantic or beautiful (card)
After any card: Love, passion, intensity

Queen of Cups

Queen of Cups

The Queen of Cups is virtuous and kind. A loving parent to everyone in the realm, the Queen sits quietly upon the throne, protecting all that there is with loyalty, intuition, and wisdom.

Upright, the Queen is the purest of heart. Reversed, typically this card is about a treacherous or vindictive person. Either way, this card is about emotions and passions and their many sides.

The Queen of Cups as:

An action?
- Be a good listener
- Join a nonprofit board
- Help someone

Place in your house?
- The phone or other communication device

Place in your city?
- A psychotherapy office
- A school

Place in the world?
- The Greek isles
- Great Britain
- The Great Lakes

Something to eat?
- Comfort food
- Eat at home rather than out

A color? Purple

A movie theme? Empathy, mother's love
- Freaky Friday
- Sister Act
- Three Billboards outside Ebbing, Missouri

A new career?
- Doctor
- Nurse
- Counselor
- Lounge singer

Questions answered by Queen of Cups:

Who? A psychotherapist; a good listener
What? A heart
Where? A lake
When? Mid-June to Mid-July; In due time
Why? We all need to understand our own emotions
Yes or No? It depends on emotional control

What should I clean?
- The office desk
- Your social media follow list

Where are my keys?
- Near water

Queen of Cups combinations

With Hermit: You've done all you can, now it is time to be alone with your feelings and intuition.
With Five of Wands: A tough fight leads to emotional distress - take time out.
With Four of Cups: Someone who seemingly does not care may just need an emotional break - give them space.
With King of Swords: A disciplined and headstrong person softens with love and compassion.
With Three of Pentacles: A nonprofit organization. Collaborating with heart is the best way to build a business.

Before any card: Be empathetic to (card)
After any card: Love, sincerity, empathy

King of Cups

The King of Cups is a mature person who leads with the heart, not the head. On a regular basis, this King appreciates the finer things, such as drinking a top shelf liquor while admiring their beautiful possessions.

The King is warm-hearted and calm, perhaps a lawyer in a nonprofit sector, or someone's favorite teacher.

The King of Cups as:

An action?
- Channel your passions into something creative
- Start a new hobby

Place in your house?
- Dad's chair
- The piano or wherever instruments are kept

Place in your city?
- A music school
- A nonprofit organization

Place in the world?
- Mexico
- British Columbia
- Camping
- Augusta

Something to eat?
- BBQ seafood
- A fine liqueur

A color? blue

A movie theme? healer, father's love
- Father of the Bride
- Beauty and the Beast
- Patch Adams

A new career?
- Counselor
- Teacher
- Curator
- Mediator or Facilitator

Questions answered by King of Cups:

Who? A mediator or lawyer; A parent
What? A musical instrument
Where? The sea
When? Mid-February to Mid-March; Mid October to Mid-November; in a while
Why? Professional guidance is important
Yes or No? Maybe. Some advice may be needed

What should I clean?
- The music room
- The living room

Where are my keys?
- In Dad's chair
- Near a piano

King of Cups combinations

With Wheel of Fortune: The balance of power is in your control - maintain calm.
With Three of Wands: What you dream of will happen, but it will take strength, compassion, and a lot of patience.
With Page of Cups: The apple does not fall far from the tree.
With Ten of Swords: Defeat or failure creates a more empathetic and caring person.
With Two of Pentacles: Change is inevitable, so prioritize what is important to you.

Before any card: Take a diplomatic and calm approach to (card)
After any card: compassion, diplomacy

Swords

Swords represent fire, knowledge, and the internal conflict we have in our own mind.

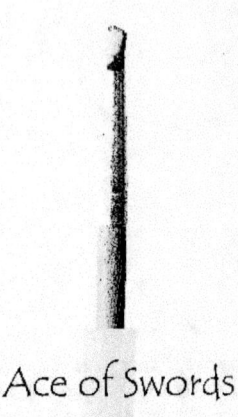

Ace of Swords

Ace of Swords

One of the most positive swords cards in the deck, the Ace represents a strong element of determination, intelligence, and focus. It may suggest a victory using the mind or one's wits.
Occasionally, the conflict and resulting win represented by the Ace of Swords is an internal battle, rather than an external one.

The Ace of Swords as:

An action?
- Solve a problem
- Do a puzzle to exercise your gray matter
- Focus on your project

Place in your house?
- A puzzle or problem
- The air conditioning unit

Place in your city?
- The library
- The courts
- An overpass
- A bridge

Place in the world?
- Hong Kong
- Japan
- London
- New York
- The Bay Area

Something to eat?
- Coffee
- Turmeric
- Spices

A color? white

A movie theme? Clarity
- A Beautiful Mind
- The Imitation Game

A new career?
- Legal work
- Mental work
- Law enforcement
- Blacksmith

Questions answered by Ace of Swords:

Who? The smartest
What? A paper airplane; a puzzle
Where? In the air
When? Now; December through March - The entire season of Winter (Northern Hemisphere) or Summer (Southern Hemisphere)
Why? The truth is out there
Yes or No? Yes

What should I clean?
- Dust high shelves, fan blades, or blinds

Where are my keys?
- Somewhere smart
- Up high

Ace of Swords combinations

With Hierophant: A sharp-witted and ethical person knows what to do.
With Three of Wands: Keep your head clear and your eyes on the prize.
With Six of Cups: Think fondly about happy memories and how to recreate them.
With Ten of Swords: Complete failure leads to mental clarity and a breakthrough on the next project.
With Ace of Pentacles: A clear head and intense focus leads to a new and prosperous opportunity.

Before any card: Obtaining wisdom about (card)
After any card: Knowledge, clarity

Two of Swords

The Two represents an equal distribution of forces in opposition to each other. It may indicate a dilemma with no clear path forward, a decision with no right or wrong choice, or two paths - neither of which is better than the other.
In any situation, just choosing a course of action helps alleviate distress.

The Two of Swords as:

An action?
- Decide something and don't look back
- Choose a direction and start driving or hiking

Place in your house?
- A windowsill
- A banister
- A hallway with two directions

Place in your city?
- A crosswalk
- An overpass
- A major intersection

Place in the world?
- Wall Street
- Minneapolis - St. Paul
- A capital city
- Gibraltar Airport
- This Way and That Way, Lake Jackson, TX

Something to Eat?
- Reese peanut butter cups
- Pineapple Pizza
- A new and different food combination

A color? Grey

A movie theme? Indecision
- Sliding Doors
- Definitely, Maybe
- Hamlet

A new career?
- Scientist
- Hairdresser
- Ninja, sensei

Questions answered by Two of Swords:

Who? The decision maker; The most confused person
What? A set of knives
Where? Twin Cities
When? The end of September; Two days from now
Why? Remaining indecisive is not an option
Yes or No? Maybe

What should I clean?
- The windows
- The knives

Where are my keys?
- On a precarious ledge
- The cutlery drawer

Two of Swords combinations

With Lovers: A difficult decision must be made regarding a partner.
With Page of Wands: There are many options - do not get weighed down by them all.
With Five of Cups: After the decision is made, there is regret over the unpicked options - keep looking forward instead.
With Nine of Swords: Anxiety over a difficult choice may lead to a stalemate.
With King of Pentacles: If King precedes, avoid indecision about how to manage your wealth. If King follows, deciding now will lead to prosperity.

Before any card: A choice about (card)
After any card: indecision and questions

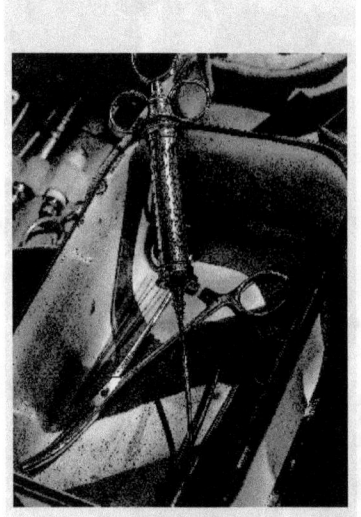
Three of Swords

Three of Swords

This is a card of pain and sorrow. The three bloody swords indicate that the head has won over the heart, and the result is loss or devastation. It could be the end of a job or relationship, an accidental injury or death, or something else causing deep and difficult grief.

After despair comes a new beginning, but you must face the grief head on in order to push through it.

The Three of Swords as:

An action?
- Make a sacrifice in order to recover
- Acknowledge hurt
- Go *through* the pain, not around it

Place in your house?
- A keepsake that brings melancholy
- Ashes
- Cobwebs

Place in your city?
- The cemetery
- The mausoleum
- A war memorial

Place in the world?
- Afghanistan
- Syria
- Auschwitz
- Dubrovnik

Something to eat?
- Nightshade plants
- Soda
- Greek yogurt

A color? Grey, red

A movie theme? Loss, sorrow, unwanted truth
- Steel Magnolias
- The Hate U Give
- Ghost

A new career?
- Heart surgeon
- Counselor
- Butcher
- Poacher
- Farmer

Questions answered by Three of Swords:

Who? The ex; Someone grieving a terrible loss
What? A dead body; The end
Where? A grave
When? The beginning of October; Now; Three units of time from now
Why? Failure is the greatest teacher
Yes or No? No

What should I clean?
- Tidy up clutter that makes you sad
- The memorial items
- The shelf with the ashes

Where are my keys?
- Where you lost them (Sorry, this card is terrible)

Three of Swords combinations

With World: (3 before World) Total heartbreak eventually leads to fulfillment, or (3 after World) the loss of all you hold dear.
With Queen of Wands: You possess the courage required to face the heartbreak, plan your way through the stages of grief.
With Four of Cups: Failure or loss leads to apathy and disconnectedness.
With Eight of Swords: You are imprisoned in your own heartbreak - get help.
With Knight of Pentacles: Pain leads to a greater sense of responsibility.

Before any card: Tragedy surrounding (card)
After any card: Loss, sorrow, despair

Four of Swords

After the dark and upsetting three comes a period of rest and contemplation. The four of swords is about withdrawal and retreat, perhaps temporary, so you can recover.

When the four does not follow a painful experience, it might indicate that there is a delay in plans, or that things may not be going quite as expected.

The Four of Swords as:

An action?
- Take a nap
- Meditate

Place in your house?
- The sofa
- A hammock
- A bed

Place in your city?
- A church
- A break room
- A massage studio

Place in the world?
- Thailand
- Bali
- Portugal
- The Maldives

Something to eat?
- Ginger or chamomile tea
- Almonds
- Nuts

A color? grey, yellow

A movie theme? Rest, mental work
- Eat, Pray, Love
- Frozen
- Sleeping Beauty

A new career?
- Mattress tester
- Quilter
- Non-medical roles in the health care industry
- Hospitality and tourism

Questions answered by Four of Swords:

Who? The sleepiest; a therapist
What? A nap
Where? A bed
When? The middle of October; Afterwards; Four days from now
Why? Requiring rest is not a weakness.
Yes or No? A mild yes

What should I clean?
- Don't clean, take a nap instead
- Fluff the pillows

Where are my keys?
- The last place you were lying down

Four of Swords combinations

With Chariot: Restore yourself by maintaining control of your thoughts.
With King of Wands: A great leader overcomes challenges through retrospection and patience.
With Three of Cups: A restorative getaway vacation with friends, such as a camping trip or retreat.
With Seven of Swords: Taking a nap feels devious but may be exactly what you need to think of new strategies.
With Queen of Pentacles: A practical and secure person needs to contemplate an idea a little while longer; Mom needs a nap.

Before any card: meditate on (card)
After any card: nap, rest, serious consideration

Five of Swords

Five of Swords

The swords are never at rest for long. The Five represents the time after a battle or conflict. If it is a victory, it is an empty one. If it's a defeat, it requires a major regroup and re-plan.

In the Rider-Waite, a person stands holding the swords they have acquired in battle, but they have lost their comrades in the meantime. While at first it appears to be a win, the card itself represents nothing but discord and trouble.

The Five of Swords as:

An action?
- Change your dysfunctional habits.
- Collect your knives or tools in one place

Place in your house?
- The bar
- A child's room
- A competitive game

Place in your city?
- Parking garage
- Traffic

Place in the world?
- Stalingrad/Volgograd Russia
- Waterloo, France
- Persia
- Argentina
- A place of great defeat

Something to eat?
- Bananas
- Rice
- Soda crackers
- Breakroom snacks

A color? grey, green

A movie theme? defeat, arguments
- Fight Club
- The War of the Roses
- The Money Pit

A new career?
- Investigator
- Insurance assessor
- Gambler
- Multi-level marketing

Questions answered by Five of Swords:

Who? Either the defeated, or a winner who is not proud of his or her victory
What? A fight
Where? A boxing ring
When? The end of January; After a battle; Five units of time from now
Why? Winning is not the most important thing right now
Yes or No? No

What should I clean?
- A playroom or child's room
- The knives
- The tools

Where are my keys?
- Where you had your last argument

Five of Swords combinations

With Strength: This may be a rare time where a fight needs to happen, be brave and compassionate.
With Knight of Wands: Jumping in with uncontrolled ambition will lead to a hollow victory.
With Two of Cups: An argument with your partner goes nowhere and is disappointing.
With Six of Swords: After a conflict there is a long and arduous adjustment.
With Two of Pentacles: Before you start a battle, weigh the pros and cons carefully - there is more at stake than anticipated.

Before any card: A battle over (card)
After any card: defeat, empty victory

Six of Swords

Six of Swords

The Six depicts a gradual change or difficult journey. This is a troublesome trip, and one that is not wanted but is absolutely necessary for survival.

In most decks, a family paddles a ship across the sea, huddled with only the clothes on their back and each other.

The Six of Swords is about a painful but necessary transition.

The Six of Swords as:

An action?
- Move on
- Water travel
- Change your location

Place in your house?
- The closet
- A bathroom
- A room being renovated

Place in your city?
- Bridge
- Canal
- Marina
- Crossroads
- A freeway out of town

Place in the world?
- Portugal
- Berlin
- Helsinki
- Columbia

Something to eat?
- baked instead of au gratin potatoes
- Romaine instead of iceberg
- *Eat This, Not That*[10]

A color? grey, blue

A movie theme? a difficult journey
- Poseidon
- National Lampoon's Vacation
- Planes, Trains and Automobiles

A new career?
- Travel industry
- Cruise employee
- A job in another city

---

[10] Eat This, Not That (David Zincenzko, 2014)

Questions answered by Six of Swords:

Who? Someone undergoing a huge transition
What? A necessary trip
Where? A boat
When? The first week in February; Six weeks from now
Why? Great relief is on the other side of difficulty
Yes or No? If you make the necessary changes, yes

What should I clean?
- A closet
- The tub
- The boat

Where are my keys?
- Where you last changed your clothes

Six of Swords combinations

With Hermit: You may need more time alone to contemplate big changes.
With Seven of Wands: You're being defensive about your next big transition - why?
With Ace of Cups: New emotions lead to an important situational change.
With King of Swords: The logical move is to change course; A knowledgeable person knows they need to make a difficult transition.
With Ace of Pentacles: On the other side of a difficult journey is a new and amazing opportunity.

Before any card: A difficult transition involving (card)
After any card: Travel, leaving behind

Seven of Swords

Seven of Swords

The Seven of Swords is about stealth, manipulation, and getting away with something sneaky. In the Rider-Waite, a young person is running away with a collection of presumably stolen swords, glancing over a shoulder to make sure no one sees.
The person represented by the Seven knows they are doing something wrong, but they are doing it anyway.

The Seven of Swords as:

An action?
- Steal away for a minute
- Get away with something
- Move seven things

Place in your house?
- The back patio
- The locks on all the doors

Place in your city?
- A bank
- An amusement park

Place in the world?
- London
- Antwerp
- Turkey

Something to eat?
- Cheese
- Kobe Beef
- Your coworker's lunch

A color? Yellow

A movie theme? Thievery, crime
- Catch Me If You Can
- Home Alone

A new career?
- Spy
- Thief
- Secret Service
- Transport driver
- Copyright lawyer

Questions answered by Seven of Swords:

Who? A trickster
What? A robbery
Where? A vault
When? The middle of February; Seven days
Why? Sometimes a bit of manipulation is called for, but be mindful of who gets hurt
Yes or No? Probably not

What should I clean?
- The valuables
- Polish the doorknobs

Where are my keys?
- Where you last got away with something sneaky
- Somebody has hidden them from you

Seven of Swords combinations

With Wheel of Fortune: Be strategic in your tricks - karma has a way of exposing deviance.
With Four of Wands: A deception takes place at home.
With King of Cups: An otherwise loving adult has a trick up their sleeve.
With Knight of Swords: A thief or trickster dives right in, but impulsivity might spoil the plan.
With Ten of Pentacles: A legacy of deception is left behind; The culmination of deviance might have met its end.

Before any card: Getting away with (card)
After any card: Thievery or manipulation

Eight of Swords

Eight of Swords

Commonly depicted on the Eight is a person tied and blindfolded, surrounded by eight swords stuck in the ground. The person feels helpless and is afraid to move.

However, the blindfold and ropes are a metaphor for the person's own fears. If they would just take a moment to gain perspective, they would see that they are not bound tightly at all, and that there is a way out of the cage.

The Eight of Swords is about breaking free of self-victimization and finding your way out of a bad situation.

The Eight of Swords as:

An action?
- Break free
- Trim a hedge
- Clear a path through clutter

Place in your house?
- Under stair storage
- The basement
- The attic

Place in your city?
- A jail cell
- A train station
- Traffic
- A busy mall

Place in the world?
- Cuba
- China
- Alcatraz
- Hanoi

Something to eat?
- Pigs in a blanket
- Corn dog
- Bacon wrapped filet mignon
- Egg in a hole

A color? grey, blue

A movie theme? prison, helplessness
- 12 Monkeys
- Jojo Rabbit
- Logan's Run

A new career?
- Special needs therapist or teacher
- Prison guard or Security officer
- Magician or escape artist
- Tailor

Questions answered by Eight of Swords:

Who? Someone who feels or is trapped
What? An excuse
Where? Your thoughts
When? The middle of May; Eight units of time; When your inner critic stops
Why? Often our limitations are self-imposed
Yes or No? no

What should I clean?
- An otherwise abandoned storage area
- A path through somewhere messy

Where are my keys?
- Trapped near water
- In a pile of clutter on the floor

Eight of Swords combinations

With Justice: Cause and effect causes feelings of entrapment, but it is likely self-victimization. Look for the truth.
With Ace of Wands: Someone stubbornly defends their position, and it could limit their ability to succeed. Move forward.
With Queen of Cups: A wise and caring helper can guide you out of trouble.
With Five of Swords: A desire to win at all costs leads to fear or loss.
With King of Pentacles: Until you break free of the chains that bind you, you may not find abundance; Also, find a new job.

Before any card: Being unable to break free of (card)
After any card: Imprisonment, self-victimization

Nine of Swords

Nine of Swords

The Nine of Swords is a card of anxiety, pain, and nightmares. While not the worst card in the deck, it is nevertheless foreboding and very rarely divines anything positive. The person in this card is agony and loss personified.

It is a difficult challenge to find practical and simple answers to a card so involved with matters inside the head - but I will try not to get too Nine of Swords about it. Clear and annotated meanings do exist for this card.

The Nine of Swords as:

An action?
- Record your dreams and nightmares
- Buy a new pillow or comforter
- Talk to a therapist

Place in your house?
- The bed
- A frightening location, like a cluttered cabinet or a dark basement that gives you the heebie-jeebies

Place in your city?
- A house of horrors
- A war memorial
- The couch at a therapist's office

Place in the world?
- Czech Republic
- Switzerland
- Liverpool
- Transylvania

Something to eat?
- Biscuits
- Spicy food
- Dark chocolate
- A gelatin salad

A color? Black, blue

A movie theme? fear, anxiety, insomnia
- Any horror film
- Spirited Away

A new career?
- Mental health therapist
- Third-shift work
- Dream interpreter
- Barista

Questions answered by Nine of Swords:

Who? The most anxious person
What? A nightmare
Where? Your dreams
When? The first week of June; Nine hours; Anxious moments
Why? Situations we do not deal with right away can haunt us later
Yes or No? Oh gosh, no. No no no

What should I clean?
- The basement
- A storage area that overwhelms you

Where are my keys?
- A place of nightmares
- A messy storage area

Nine of Swords combinations

With Hanged Man: A great sacrifice leads to anxiety and hopelessness.
With Ten of Wands: Taking on too much responsibility is a nightmare.
With Knight of Cups: A sensitive lover feels anxiety about a relationship.
With Three of Swords: Grief is overwhelming and unlivable. Seek therapy.
With Queen of Pentacles: An anxious mother or parent.

Before any card: Severe anxiety associated with (card)
After any card: Anxiety, nightmares, being frightened

Ten of Swords

Ten of Swords

There is nothing to cheer about when the Ten arrives. Upright, it is pain, destruction, defeat and a terrible end. Even reversed, it can often represent clinging to disaster and not being able to move on.

Skilled tarot interpreters are good at finding the card's positive messages, such as "there is nowhere to go but up" or "the future is bright," but in a practical and grounded sense, this card is pretty much the *worst*.

The Ten of Swords as:

An action?
- Destroy something, such as demoing a room to remodel
- Feel sorry for yourself

Place in your house?
- The first aid kit
- Where the most accidents occur

Place in your city?
- Hospice care
- A mausoleum

Place in the world?
- Humanity itself
- A place of terrible devastation

Something to eat?
- Baked pasta
- Potato casserole
- Deviled Eggs

A color? Black, grey, white

A movie theme? Rock bottom, death
- Macbeth
- Kill Bill
- Everything Must Go

A new career?
- Funeral director
- Forensics
- grief counselor
- gravesite worker

Questions answered by Ten of Swords:

Who? A dead person
What? A catastrophe
Where? The floor, the ground
When? The middle of June; Ten days; The end
Why? The situation is as bad as it could possibly be
Yes or No? No

What should I clean?
- The knives
- The silverware drawer

Where are my keys?
- Under a blanket
- On the floor

Ten of Swords combinations

With Death: Complete failure.
With Nine of Wands: Have bravery in your defeat, we learn from our mistakes.
With Page of Cups: (10 before Page) A terrible loss leads to a happy new surprise, like a baby after a miscarriage, or a great job after a layoff. (10 after Page) A happy surprise comes with problems.
With Four of Swords: Make sure you've taken proper time to recuperate after a loss.
With Knight of Pentacles: Hard work pulls you out of this defeating moment.

Before any card: The total devastation or end of (card)
After any card: Destruction, end, failure

Page of Swords

Page of Swords

Swords are air cards associated with intellect, but many of the numbered swords cards are rife with warnings, endings and pain.

It is the Page of Swords who heralds better news. The Page is the beginning of knowledge, or a fresh academic start.

Although the Page of Swords might also be stubborn and intensely opinionated, they are curious and intellectual.

The Page of Swords as:

An action?
- Learn something new
- Gossip (in a nice way, if possible)

Place in your house?
- Textbook shelf
- A homeschooling area

Place in your city?
- An elementary school
- A children's library

Place in the world?
- South Korea
- Japan
- Finland
- Ireland
- Montenegro
- Boston

Something to eat?
- Deli sandwich
- Cottage cheese or yogurt
- Fresh fruit
- Elementary school snacks

A color? Yellow

A movie theme? A studious young mind
- Eternal Sunshine of the Spotless Mind
- Accepted
- Legally Blonde

A new career?
- Communications and Informatics
- Spy
- Sales
- Something you dreamed of becoming when you were a child

Questions answered by Page of Swords:

Who? A student
What? A lesson
Where? School
When? The entire season of Winter (Northern Hemisphere), or Summer (Southern Hemisphere); The first day of class
Why? News is coming
Yes or No? Yes

What should I clean?
- Textbooks or educational area
- The office desk

Where are my keys?
- Under a book

Page of Swords combinations

With Temperance: Now is the time to find meaning in everyday things.
With Eight of Wands: A student travels by air; Curiosity leads to rapid change or movement.
With Ten of Cups: Use your mind to make your dreams a reality - plan the steps logically so that the fantasy comes true.
With Two of Swords: A difficult choice causes restlessness and impatience.
With Page of Pentacles: Two young, intelligent people start an ambitious new project.

Before any card: Learning more about (card)
After any card: Curiosity, a student

Knight of Swords

Knight of Swords

This Knight charges into battle with focus and purpose. While this person is confident and well spoken, they may also be foolhardy and impetuous.

When this card appears, there is a force on the horizon - either generated *by* you or coming *for* you. Either way, be prepared for turbulence. When the storm comes, make decisive action.

The Knight of Swords as:

An action?
- Dive into your new project
- Charge! ...your phone and other devices

Place in your house?
- A balcony or rooftop
- A teen's room

Place in your city?
- A secondary or high school
- A tall building

Place in the world?
- Denmark
- Singapore
- Switzerland

Something to eat?
- Bento box
- Rations
- Order meal delivery

A color? White, red

A movie theme? Courage, exploration
- The Revenant
- The Indiana Jones franchise
- Dead Poets Society

A new career?
- IT and Tech
- Game developer
- Combat soldier

Questions answered by Knight of Swords:

Who? A teenager
What? A bold new idea
Where? A startup company; A high school
When? Mid-January to Early February; The middle of the school year; Soon
Why? "Impatience can cause wise people to do foolish things" ~Janette Oke
Yes or No? Probably not

What should I clean?
- High shelves
- Something belonging to a teen

Where are my keys?
- Where you started a new project

Knight of Swords combinations

With Devil: Impulsivity causes one to fall into dangerous situations or addiction.
With Six of Wands: Charging in headfirst results in a victory, this time.
With Nine of Cups: Take action to defend what is important to you.
With Ace of Swords: Jump boldly into your new idea and you will gain clarity as you go.
With Ten of Pentacles: A bold adventure reaches its exciting culmination.

Before any card: Jumping boldly into (card) without considering the consequences
After any card: Ambition, or a bold new idea

Queen of Swords

Queen of Swords

The Queen of Swords is an independent, sharp-witted person, but possibly so much so that they appear distant and cold-hearted.

At the Queen's core, however, is a clear and truthful communicator, who is very self-aware, fiercely individual, and unique. This perfectionism may be a cause of pain or sorrow, however.

If not representative of yourself, then the Queen is a powerful ally to have on your side.

The Queen of Swords as:

An action?
- Write a book
- Send an email
- Tell someone the truth

Place in your house?
- Your laptop computer
- A nonfiction book

Place in your city?
- An undergraduate institution
- A teacher's college

Place in the world?
- Sweden
- Denmark
- The Netherlands
- Germany

Something to eat?
- Fried rice
- Beans and rice
- Chili

A color? white, grey

A movie theme? A sharp-witted woman
- The Devil Wears Prada
- Still Alice
- Lady Bird

A new career?
- Professor or researcher
- Doctor or Lawyer
- Critic
- Information specialist

Questions answered by Queen of Swords:

Who? A wise lady
What? A packet of educational materials
Where? College or University
When? Mid-September to early October; College; When you have learned enough
Why? Great clarity of mind will help you pursue your goals
Yes or No? Maybe

What should I clean?
- Sort and organize the bookshelves

Where are my keys?
- Near the computer, phone, or important paperwork

Queen of Swords combinations

With Tower: A sudden disaster leads to a clear head and rational planning.
With Five of Wands: A debate or conflict is on the horizon - study as much as you can before you go head to head.
With Eight of Cups: Be prepared to walk away if you cannot get through to someone logically.
With King of Swords: A powerful and ambitious couple rule with their head instead of their heart. Possibly no love in the pairing, but a marriage of convenience.
With Nine of Pentacles: A practical and logical mind leads to a luxurious and rewarding future.

Before any card: Being direct about (card)
After any card: Independence, a quick wit

King of Swords

King of Swords

The King of Swords is the professional authority on whatever matter you are dealing with.

An authentic and intelligent leader, the King is kind and helpful, but the motivation is not a friendly one - The King is here to get business done and that is it.

The King of Swords can be dominating and assertive, but they know what they are talking about. Listen.

The King of Swords as:

An action?
- Be assertive
- Engage in a civil matter
- File a lawsuit
- Contact a professional
- Write to congress

Place in your house?
- The office
- The filing cabinet

Place in your city?
- A government office
- A research university

Place in the world?
- New York
- Vienna
- Geneva
- Brussels

Something to eat?
- Coffee
- Kale
- Salmon
- Whole grains

A color? Purple, white

A movie theme? Wisdom, cold-heartedness
- Knives Out
- Murder on the Orient Express
- Clue

A new career?
- Business owner
- Doctor or lawyer
- Professor
- Upper management

Questions answered by King of Swords:

Who? A lawyer
What? An important piece of paper
Where? Grad school; A government office
When? Mid May to early June; During a legal battle; In a few years
Why? A superior intellect guides us through opposition
Yes or No? No clear answer; consult an authority

What should I clean?
- The filing cabinet
- The entire office and do not ask again until you are done

Where are my keys?
- You put them down when you brought in the mail
- On your desk

King of Swords combinations

With Star: The truth will come out after a period of respite and rejuvenation.
With Three of Wands: A startup business is on the verge of rapid growth, seek help from a lawyer or other authority.
With Seven of Cups: Someone is daydreaming about being in power.
With Three of Swords: The truth is discovered at the edge of despair.
With Eight of Pentacles: A student learns all he can from a professor and may one day be the professor themself.

Before any card: Do hard work for (card)
After any card: Business, leadership

Pentacles

Pentacles represent earth, money, and the physical and material world that we can see and touch.

Ace of Pentacles

Ace of Pentacles

The Pentacles are about earthly, physical, material things. It is money and careers, belongings and luxury, babies and nature, and everything we can touch with our physical senses.

Therefore, pulling the Ace of Pentacles in a reading is an extremely positive message about an upcoming productive or rewarding period in your life.

Because Pentacles represent so many visible aspects of our physical world, it is awfully hard to simplify the Pentacle cards down to one or two tangible items - because they represent *all* the tangible items in the world!

The Ace of Pentacles as:

An action?
- Ground yourself
- Give or receive a gift
- Do some shopping
- Sell your wares

Place in your house?
- A piggy bank
- A plant
- The baby's room

Place in your city?
- The ATM
- The supermarket
- A department store

Place in the world?
- Ethiopia
- The Amazon or Nile river
- Norway
- The Congo
- A safari

Something to eat?
- Corn or Maize
- Roots, seeds, berries

A color? Earth tones

A movie theme? Opportunity, investing
- The Big Short
- The Producers
- The Social Network

A new career?
- Property owner or real estate worker
- Landscaper or gardener
- Retail cashier, restaurant busboy
- business startup

Questions answered by Ace of Pentacles:

Who? A baby
What? A gift; A dollar
Where? In the garden
When? Now; Spring (Northern Hemisphere) or Autumn (Southern Hemisphere)
Why? It is time to strengthen your roots
Yes or No? Yes

What should I clean?
- Water the plants
- Bathe the baby

Where are my keys?
- Near your money

Ace of Pentacles combinations

With Moon: Prosperity comes at the end of a long and arduous journey. Trust your intuition.
With Two of Wands: A new adult leaves the home to venture out on their own.
With Knight of Cups: A romantic fool dives in - a new relationship is born.
With Page of Swords: A curious mind finds treasure.
With Seven of Pentacles: Keep persevering - rewards are coming soon; tangible results may be apparent at the end of May.

Before any card: A gift involving (card)
After any card: Shopping, investing, new acquisitions

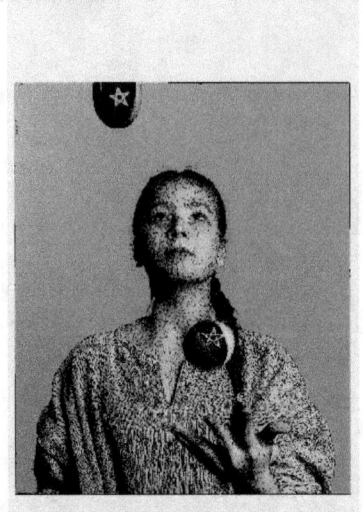

Two of Pentacles

Two of Pentacles

    The Two of Pentacles is about balancing your resources. For many people it takes a fair amount of juggling to cover all the bills but still eat for the month. Finding that critical financial balance is what the two is all about.
    For those who are not as stressed over covering bills, the Two of Pentacles might represent exchanging goods, transferring funds between accounts, or the basic economics of everyday life.
    In all situations, it is about weighing material goods and finding a solution that works in any situation.

The Two of Pentacles as:

An action?
- Learn to Juggle
- Pay the bills

Place in your house?
- A kitchen or bathroom scale
- An online banking site

Place in your city?
- The circus
- A wave pool
- A bill payee

Place in the world?
- Montreal
- Las Vegas
- Monaco
- The Caribbean
- Sweden

Something to eat?
- Apples
- Oranges

A color? Blue, red

A movie theme? juggling, adaptability
- A Bug's Life
- The Greatest Showman
- Ant-Man

A new career?
- Entertainer
- Circus performer
- Games industry
- Librarian
- Admin or accountant

Questions answered by Two of Pentacles:

Who? A juggler; Someone trying to balance several parts of his or her life
What? Balls
Where? At a playpark
When? The end of December; Two days from now; When balance occurs
Why? Sometimes we need to balance more than one ball in the air
Yes or No? Too many fluctuating pieces; Maybe, maybe not

What should I clean?
- The bathroom
- The toys

Where are my keys?
- Perched precariously somewhere high up

Two of Pentacles combinations

With Sun: Prioritizing now leads to success, there are no wrong answers.
With Page of Wands: An exciting new opportunity requires balancing one's current lifestyle first.
With Queen of Cups: A loving and generous person must choose.
With Ten of Swords: After a complete failure or upheaval, one can adapt to the change.
With Six of Pentacles: Choose a charity to donate to - do your research first.

Before any card: Juggling or prioritizing (card)
After any card: Balance, juggling, options

Three of Pentacles

Three of Pentacles

    The Three of Pentacles is a card of collaboration and mastery, artistic ability, and teamwork. A ball player cannot win without a team. A skilled worker cannot complete the job without the help of coworkers who may be there to contribute, teach, or just tell the worker if the art being hung is level.
    The Three is about the teamwork required to get the job done.

The Three of Pentacles as:

An action?
- Do a home project such as painting or changing a lightbulb
- Invite a friend to help with a project
- Collaborate with experts

Place in your house?
- A project room
- The workshop
- Up on a wall

Place in your city?
- A garage
- A gallery
- A building supply company

Place in the world?
- Egypt
- South Africa
- Italy
- France

Something to eat?
- Bagels
- Something you made or ordered with a friend

A color? grey, brown

A movie theme? Collaboration, apprenticeship
- The Avengers franchise
- Zootopia
- Ghostbusters

A new career?
- Architect
- Construction
- Laborer
- Painter
- Interior designer

Questions answered by Three of Pentacles:

Who? A tradesperson or trades student
What? A poured foundation; concrete
Where? Standing on a bench
When? The beginning of January; When you start working on a new skill
Why? You still have a lot to learn
Yes or No? Yes

What should I clean?
- The kitchen
- Complete a project that is bugging you

Where are my keys?
- Where you started your last project

Three of Pentacles combinations

With Judgement: Start learning that new skill or working on that new project.
With Queen of Wands: A mature person helps one continue their work.
With Seven of Cups: "Teamwork Makes the Dream Work![11]"
With Nine of Swords: There is a lot of anxiety about starting something new - seek therapy or assistance.
With Five of Pentacles: One has trouble reaching out for help.

Before any card: Collaborating on (card)
After any card: Teamwork, study, building

---

[11] This well-known phrase is first attributed to John Maxwell, an American Clergyman. His original quote was "Teamwork makes the dream work, but a vision becomes a nightmare when the leader has a big dream and a bad team."

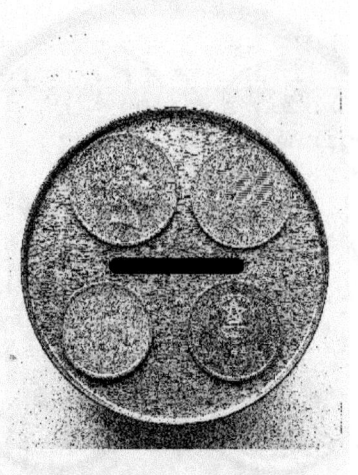

Four of Pentacles

Four of Pentacles

The Four of Pentacles is the money lover, one who clutches at material goods and does not let go. The person represented by the four may be opposed to sharing, or perhaps they come from an impoverished background and do not want to lose their sense of security again.

Although this card represents a pleasant chapter of your life where your needs are met, it is also a warning not to be selfish about what you have acquired.

The Four of Pentacles as:

An action?
- Check your credit report and accounts
- Move more into savings

Place in your house?
- Your prized goods
- Your money
- The mattress

Place in your city?
- A financial services industry
- The stock market
- the bank

Place in the world?
- The coast
- The Ozarks
- Columbia
- The Caribbean

Something to eat?
- Fine dining
- Food that cannot be shared

A color? grey, yellow

A movie theme? protecting resources
- Wall Street
- Weekend at Bernie's
- Parasite

A new career?
- Finance, retirement investment, or accounting
- New business development
- Collector
- Environmental conservationist

Questions answered by Four of Pentacles:

Who? A tightwad
What? A stash of cash
Where? In a purse, pocket, or wallet
When? The middle of January; When you have earned enough money
Why? You have a firm foundation, so do not fear change
Yes or No? Yes

What should I clean?
- Your room

Where are my keys?
- Near you - possibly in your pocket

Four of Pentacles combinations

With The World: Fulfillment and security has been reached, now share with the world what you have received.
With King of Wands: A conservative leader has trouble sharing the wealth, such as a boss who will not issue pay raises.
With Page of Cups: A sensitive and dreamy young person gets a lesson in conserving his or her resources.
With Eight of Swords: Someone is unable to see a path to wealth, but they may be imposing their own restrictions upon themselves.
With Ace of Pentacles: A new job with more benefits and pay is available

Before any card: Conservation of (card)
After any card: Greed, security, hoarding

Five of Pentacles

The Five of Pentacles appears daunting and ominous, but there is opportunity in this card as well. The impoverished person who is stuck outside in the cold need only to look around, and will see a light shining from a warm, secure, and welcoming place for the night.

The five is about looking for these opportunities when you are feeling unstable. It is also about changing from a mindset of scarcity to gratitude.

The Five of Pentacles as:

An action?
- Look behind you
- Ask for help
- Get a health checkup

Place in your house?
- A shrine
- The phone
- A window to something that brings you joy

Place in your city?
- A church
- A shelter
- A hotel

Place in the world?
- Canada
- Yemen
- Australia
- D.R

Something to eat?
- Lentil soup
- Porridge
- Carrots and potatoes

A color? Black, white

A movie theme? Poverty, lack of stability
- Moonlight
- Les Misérables
- Hunt for the Wilderpeople

A new career?
- Social work
- Health care or medical supplier
- Solving the poverty crisis
- Stained glass artist

Questions answered by Five of Pentacles:

Who? A self-victimized person
What? A comfortable place to sleep
Where? Behind you; In the sheets
When? The end of April; When you stop complaining about resources
Why? You are not alone; you need only reach out and find people to help
Yes or No? No

What should I clean?
- The front hall closet
- The windows
- Shovel the driveway

Where are my keys?
- Behind you
- On a window ledge

Five of Pentacles combinations

With Judgment: A time of reckoning is upon you - seek help now.
With Knight of Wands: Jumping in with fearlessness may lead to insecurity, first check to make sure your bases are covered.
With Ten of Cups: The happiest person you know may be suffering internally - reach out to them.
With Seven of Swords: A trickster or thief acts this way out of necessity without knowing resources are out there for them.
With Four of Pentacles: A person is so greedy they risk losing companions.

Before any card: Worry and insecurity about (card)
After any card: A dark night, poverty

Six of Pentacles

Six of Pentacles

After the greediness of the four and the impoverishment of the five, the Six of Pentacles brings us to a position where we either have enough to give back, or we are finally open to receiving gifts.

Whether you are the giver or the receiver will depend on where you are in your life, but in either situation the six is about generosity and favors.

Therefore, even if you must be the recipient in this scenario, remember there are always ways you can help others, too.

The Six of Pentacles as:

An action?
- Donate to a charity
- Give someone a gift

Place in your house?
- The kitchen
- A pile of things to be donated

Place in your city?
- A thrift store
- A nonprofit
- An investment firm

Place in the world?
- Myanmar
- San Jose
- Philadelphia
- Switzerland

Something to eat?
- Energy bars
- Lasagna or a pasta casserole
- Tuna
- A Thanksgiving meal

A color? red, purple

A movie theme? generosity, giving
- The Grinch
- It Could Happen to You
- Pay it Forward
- Robin Hood

A new career?
- Philanthropist
- Broker or loan officer
- famous actor
- teacher or lecturer

Questions answered by Six of Pentacles:

Who? A generous person
What? A donation
Where? In someone else's possession
When? The Beginning of May; When you help someone else; Six days
Why? What you give to the world, you receive back in kind
Yes or No? Yes

What should I clean?
- Take out the garbage or recycling
- Donate clothes

Where are my keys?
- You handed them to someone

Six of Pentacles combinations

With The Sun: "Sharing is caring." When you give of yourself, you are rewarded with joy and success.
With Seven of Wands: Don't give up before your efforts are rewarded.
With Nine of Cups: Share what you have, even if it is just a laugh, with others.
With Six of Swords: A difficult experience leads to a more generous nature.
With Three of Pentacles: A nonprofit organization fulfills their generous mission. Join a nonprofit board.

Before any card: Be generous with (card)
After any card: Gifts, generosity, donation

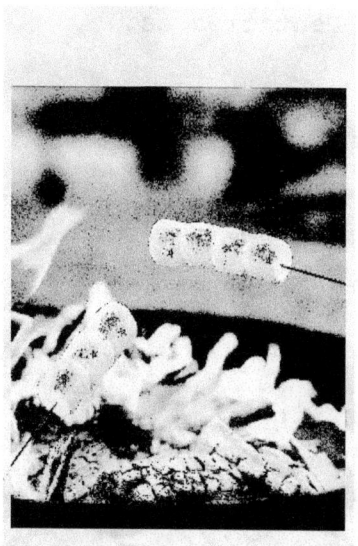

Seven of Pentacles

Seven of Pentacles

The Seven of Pentacles is about planting the seeds that will grow into success. It is patience and setbacks, but it is also perseverance and hard work.

When the Seven appears, the querent should know that wealth and prosperity are around the corner, but they must put in some hard work, and the results may be slow to come in.

This is a card about patience, assessment, and progress.

The Seven of Pentacles as:

An action?
- Plant seeds
- Buy a plant

Place in your house?
- The garden
- The plants
- The window ledge

Place in your city?
- A garden nursery
- A botanical garden

Place in the world?
- Japan
- Australia
- The Panama Canal
- The Northwest Passage
- Botanical gardens

Something to eat?
- Homemade bread
- Pot roast
- Soufflé

A color? green, yellow, orange

A movie theme? Patience, perseverance
- Forrest Gump
- Black Widow
- Serendipity

A new career?
- Gardener or outside work
- Go back to school to master a subject
- Nonprofit work

Questions answered by Seven of Pentacles:

Who? A gardener
What? A packet of seeds
Where? In the yard
When? The middle of May; After you've started the project; Seven weeks from now
Why? plans need to be assessed before, during, and after
Yes or No? Maybe later; no definitive answer yet

What should I clean?
- Vacuum the floors

Where are my keys?
- The kitchen counter
- You put them down last time you were thinking seriously about something

Seven of Pentacles combinations

With The Moon: The work seems difficult, but that might be all in your head. Get started.
With Four of Wands: The journey is halfway through; or take a break at home.
With Eight of Cups: Giving up because the work is too hard.
With Knight of Swords: A studious person dives in before assessing the work that needs to be done.
With Two of Pentacles: It is time to stand back and prioritize problems; all things in balance, including work projects.

Before any card: Plan carefully for (card)
After any card: Patience, assessment, gardening

Eight of Pentacles

Eight of Pentacles

The Eight is a skilled craftsperson or apprentice. It could represent a student completing his or her PhD, a hobbyist finishing a project, or a laborer completing a daily task.

In any situation, the Eight is about patience, hard work, and pride over one's accomplishments. Success is just around the corner, and although it may not result in financial reward, it is satisfying enough to have completed a hard day's work.

The Eight of Pentacles as:

An action?
- Work on a hobby
- Finish a project
- Study or master a subject

Place in your house?
- A studio or workshop
- A project

Place in your city?
- An art studio
- A crafts shop
- Continuing education

Place in the world?
- Mexico
- Botswana
- Greece
- Italy

Something to eat?
- Decorated cake
- Food art
- A well-plated dish
- Michelin star or James Beard award-winning restaurant

A color? Brown, yellow

A movie theme? Hard work, graduation
- Julie and Julia
- UHF
- Booksmart

A new career?
- Apprentice
- Gig and commissions artist
- Develop a new skill
- Trainer or educator

Questions answered by Eight of Pentacles:

Who? A grad student
What? A completed project
Where? In a classroom
When? The end of August; As the project ends; 8 years
Why? perseverance and focus leads to fulfilling work
Yes or No? Yes

What should I clean?
- Your workspace
- A crafts area

Where are my keys?
- Your desk

Eight of Pentacles combinations

With The Star: Have faith that finishing your project will lead to reward.
With Ace of Wands: A promotion at work!
With Seven of Cups: Someone is searching for a life's purpose; it involves skills they already possess.
With Five of Swords: An apprentice or student possesses unbridled ambition, perhaps too much. Stay focused on mastery.
With King of Pentacles: A skilled and successful person shares their knowledge.

Before any card: Study (card)
After any card: Apprenticeship, study

Bonus book recommendation:
- *Educated*, by Tara Westover

Nine of Pentacles

Nine of Pentacles

The Nine depicts a successful person on a large property surrounded by luxury. The person in the Nine has obtained great material status and comfort and keeps their power under control (In the Rider-Waite deck, a falcon is at the woman's command rather than being a predator.)

This card denotes abundance, wisdom, and the obtainment of material goods, but it might also indicate a lack of a companion to share those goods with.

The Nine of Pentacles as:

An action?
- Be thankful
- Treat yo' self[12]
- Share the wealth

Place in your house?
- Your photos
- The fridge
- The garden
- The bird's cage

Place in your city?
- A fine dining restaurant
- A market
- The zoo

Place in the world?
- Hong Kong
- Singapore
- Zurich
- Tel Aviv
- The Forbidden City

Something to eat?
- Grapes
- A catered meal
- Fruit you picked yourself

A color? Green

A movie theme? Luxury, earned rewards
- Crazy Rich Asians
- Trading Places
- Emma, Clueless

A new career?
- Fitness trainer
- Freelance work
- Custom designs
- Falconer or Aviary work
- Environmental conservationist

---

[12] From Parks and Recreation, NBC.

Questions answered by Nine of Pentacles:

Who? A wealthy person
What? A profitable skill
Where? In a palace or room of luxury
When? The beginning of September; After success is achieved; 9 months
Why? to become more self-reliant
Yes or No? Yes

What should I clean?
- Yourself! Take some time to pamper or treat yourself

Where are my keys?
- On your person, or where you put the things you just bought for yourself
- A bird got them

Nine of Pentacles combinations

With The Tower: A great upheaval leads to luxurious success.
With Ten of Wands: A fancy lifestyle is too much of a burden.
With Six of Cups: The children are one's greatest reward.
With Queen of Swords: A sharp and skilled person reaps the fruits of her labor.
With Ace of Pentacles: A new job opportunity leads to great rewards.

Before any card: Have gratitude for (card)
After any card: Luxuries, self-sufficiency

Ten of Pentacles

Ten of Pentacles

The Ten of Pentacles is about fortune, legacy, and inheritance. One has perhaps acquired such an abundance of riches or skills that they have chosen to start giving it away philanthropically, or they have passed it down to future generations.

This card depicts the epitome of wealth, the highest level of career success, or a completed family tree.

The Ten of Pentacles as:

An action?
- Enjoy what you have
- Write your will
- Channel your ancestors for wisdom

Place in your house?
- Photos of your family
- A secure place to relax

Place in your city?
- A senior center
- Your lawyer's office
- a market
- a place of wealth, legacy

Place in the world?
- Monaco
- Japan
- Hong Kong
- Iceland
- San Marino

Something to eat?
- An heirloom recipe
- Fruits

A color? yellow, red

A movie theme? Legacy, inheritance
- Brewster's Millions
- Anastasia
- Batman

A new career?
- Property developer or house flipper
- Antiques dealer
- Join the family business
- Retire

Questions answered by Ten of Pentacles:

Who? A matriarch or patriarch
What? A legacy
Where? At a financial institution
When? The middle of September; At the end; A decade
Why? success must be celebrated
Yes or No? Yes

What should I clean?
- Your bank accounts (don't clean them out, just make sure the beneficiaries are correct and things like that)
- Your heirlooms

Where are my keys?
- You may have handed them to a child

Ten of Pentacles combinations

With The Devil: Only when success has been achieved is it time to play.
With Nine of Wands: Someone takes a stand over an inheritance.
With Five of Cups: A person is sad over the legacy they have left; too many regrets to celebrate rewards.
With Four of Swords: The legacy has been passed down; it is time to rest.
With King of Pentacles: The leader of the family bequeaths a surprising inheritance.

Before any card: Pass down or share your knowledge about (card)
After any card: Inheritance, legacy, endowment

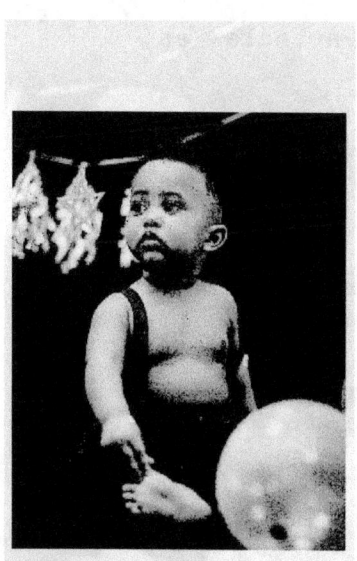

Page of Pentacles

Page of Pentacles

    The Page of Pentacles is a young, studious individual. She or he is introspective, academic, and very aware of the world in which they live, including what the planet requires for a survivable future.
    The Page may be politically active and vocal about causes that are dear to them.

The Page of Pentacles as:

An action?
- Join a protest or sign a petition
- Recycle
- Nourish your body

Place in your house?
- The front porch

Place in your city?
- A protest
- A place where young people gather
- A coffee shop

Place in the world?
- A national park
- New Orleans
- New Zealand
- the Coast

Something to eat?
- Tea
- Cream pie
- A food fight

A color? yellow, green, red

A movie theme? New student or employee
- The Breakfast Club
- Mean Girls
- Men in Black

A new career?
- Student or apprentice
- Entry-level job in a new business
- Start a new business

Questions answered by Page of Pentacles:

Who? A young, studious person
What? A new job
Where? At a park
When? Spring (Northern Hemisphere) or Fall (Southern Hemisphere); At the beginning; During class
Why? The planet needs you
Yes or No? Yes

What should I clean?
- Recycle
- Compost
- Use Earth-friendly cleaners

Where are my keys?
- You may have dropped them in the dirt

Page of Pentacles combinations

With Temperance: Go after your goals, but have patience for the length of time it might take.
With Eight of Wands: Once you choose your cause, the action is swift and decisions must be made quickly.
With Four of Cups: You are disconnected from your desires; start a dream journal.
With Two of Swords: A difficult choice must be made; Force yourself out of indecision and prosperity will start for you.
With Queen of Pentacles: A parent helps a child with a project.

Before any card: Be practical and realistic about (card)
After any card: A new job or opportunity

Knight of Pentacles

Knight of Pentacles

    Because this is a Knight, what we picture is a bold and daring adventurer, charging out to save the world, as knights tend to do.
    However, the Knight of Pentacles is more of a stationary protector. While ambitious, this knight surveys the land and chooses the best courses of action to take before making a move. With the knight's careful examination in mind, this card is about practicality and dependability.

The Knight of Pentacles as:

An action?
- Stop and assess your plans
- Read the mail
- Buy a safer car

Place in your house?
- People-watching from the front porch
- An alternate route around the house

Place in your city?
- A park bench
- Company HQ in your town
- A casual diner or favorite breakfast place

Place in the world?
- Seattle
- Austin
- Latin America
- Indonesia

Something to eat?
- Grilled cheese
- Corn chowder
- Cheese
- Vegetables

A color? Yellow, brown, red

A movie theme? Caution and practicality
- Captain America
- Priscilla, Queen of the Desert
- Gattaca

A new career?
- Routine work, like data entry
- Farmer, agriculturalist
- Handyman
- Sanitation worker, coal miner, or other government contracted labor career

Questions answered by Knight of Pentacles:

Who? An ambitious young adult
What? An idea
Where? At a new business
When? Mid-April to early May; In the early stages
Why? Starting ambitious projects requires covering one's bases
Yes or No? Yes

What should I clean?
- The workshop
- Sweep the porch or driveway

Where are my keys?
- Near the safety equipment

Knight of Pentacles combinations

With Death: The end of one project launches the beginning of a new and unexpected goal.
With Six of Wands: Hard and diligent work leads to success.
With Three of Cups: Your friends will help you achieve your goals.
With King of Swords: Think with your head, not your heart.
With Two of Pentacles: A young person must make a choice.

Before any card: Do some careful planning around (card)
After any card: Hard work, productivity

Queen of Pentacles

The Queen of Pentacles, much like the Empress in the Major Arcana, is a nurturing parent. The difference between the Queen and Empress, however, is that this queen is often a genuine human being and not an unwavering major life event that the Empress is.

This Queen is down-to-Earth, approachable, practical, and successful in business and at home. Seek out the Queen of Pentacles in your life for financial or business help.

The Queen of Pentacles as:

An action?
- Organize assets
- Streamline your business plan
- Get a business license
- Take care of the Earth

Place in your house?
- A nurturing area, such as a kitchen or baby's room

Place in your city?
- A female-owned business
- The hospital
- The supermarket
- The botanical gardens
- The Zoo

Place in the world?
- Scandinavia
- Western Europe
- Australia & New Zealand

Something to eat?
- Truffles
- Rose petals
- Food your Mom made

A color? Green, red, yellow

A movie theme? Nurturing, resourceful
- Waitress (Musical)
- Joy
- Sunshine Cleaning

A new career?
- Businesswoman or manager
- Maid, cook, or private serviceperson
- Veterinarian or zoologist
- Mom

Questions answered by Queen of Pentacles:

Who? A mother or parent; a down-to-earth businessperson
What? A new baby; a startup business
Where? At home
When? Mid December to early January; When you get back home
Why? Making practical decisions will lead to slow and steady gains
Yes or No? Definitely, yes

What should I clean?
- The kitchen
- The baby's room

Where are my keys?
- With Mom or the baby

Queen of Pentacles combinations

With Hanged Man: A sacrifice must be made in order to find financial security.
With Five of Wands: A conflict arises between the nurturer and someone else. Rise above it by providing more love.
With Two of Cups: A partnership leads to success at home and business; A romance leads to a baby.
With Knight of Swords: An impulsive person meets a practical one.
With Ace of Pentacles: An opportunity arrives to use your logical and practical mind.

Before any card: Take care of practical matters surrounding (card)
After any card: The Earth, nourishment, Mom

King of Pentacles

King of Pentacles

The King of Pentacles is a person possessing immense power, both personally and materialistically.
While a loving parent or father akin to the Queen, this person is more stubborn and has a bigger ego than the Queen counterpart. The King of Pentacles is conservative and miserly, but generous when there is a reward or thanks in it for him.

The King of Pentacles as:

An action?
- Donate to a cause
- Offer someone advice

Place in your house?
- The comfy chair

Place in your city?
- A thriving business
- A restaurant
- A sports center or arena

Place in the world?
- Mexico City
- Chicago
- Cuba
- Thailand

Something to eat?
- Fresh meat you hunted yourself
- Food that grows on vines, such as grapes, wine, tomatoes, kiwis

A color? Green, yellow, purple

A movie theme? Success, stubbornness
- Free Solo
- King Kong
- Evan Almighty

A new career?
- Businessman or general contractor
- Team owner
- Management
- Dad

Questions answered by King of Pentacles:

Who? A dad or parent; A business owner
What? A bank account; a store of luxury goods
Where? At work
When? Mid-August to early September; When the business is in the black
Why? Because you need to be careful with your resources
Yes or No? Yes

What should I clean?
- The den
- The living room

Where are my keys?
- With Dad or the kids

King of Pentacles combinations

With Justice: Being honest in business leads to abundance.
With Four of Wands: "Alone we can do so little; together we can do so much"[13]
With Ace of Cups: Following your heart leads to security and prosperity.
With Queen of Swords: A complicated person and a pragmatist form a successful partnership.
With Ace of Pentacles: When you think you have given enough, give more.

Before any card: A business involving (card)
After any card: Business, environment, Dad

---

[13] Helen Keller

Acknowledgements

I am a skilled procrastinator, which is why I use Tarot cards every day - I need them to tell me what to do! However, Tarot cards can only motivate a person so much. This book would not exist without the interminable, overwhelming, and sometimes *verbally forceful* encouragement of a few key people.

Tammy Deschamps, Amanda, Masen, Teresa, and fellow writers in the Speculative Fiction writing group. They welcomed me with open arms even though I took a break from spec-fic to write this reference.

Mindi, Rhiannon, Jon, Kelli, John, and everyone in the Cascade Writers nonprofit organization and conferences. Although we met writing fiction, their support of my nonfiction work is immeasurable.

Della Maiolo, Silvana Deurbrouck, Erin Dawson, Sharon Thomas, and all my friends and family who subjected themselves to random tarot spreads along the way.

Last but foremost, my benevolent and magnanimous[15] husband Oscar, and my three brilliant children Margaret, David, and Jack, for their gifts of time, love, and inspiration.

---

[15] I'd left adjectives for him out of the first draft, but Oscar wanted some, too.

Image Credits

All Images used in this book were obtained from Unsplash.com and altered or edited with permission by Emily Paper

The Fool - Sergey Gimburg & Alexander Dummer
The Magician - Gabe Pierce
The High Priestess - Purnachandra Rao Podilapu
The Empress - Omid Armin
The Emperor - Valeria Zoncoll
The Hierophant - Walter Gadea-Zesab
The Lovers - Travis Grossen
The Chariot - Blake Meyer
Strength - Mohamed Nohassi
The Hermit - Charles Deluvi
Wheel of Fortune - Emma Roordarl
Justice - Bady Abbas
The Hanged Man - Annie Spratt
Death - Marcos Paulo-Prado
Temperance - Kelli McClintock
The Devil - Jomjakkapat Parrueng
The Tower - Ryan Fields
The Star - Lubomirkin
The Moon - Daiga Ellaby
The Sun - Gabby Orcutt & marko Blazevi
Judgement - Kate Indra
The World - Christian Bowen & Danielle Gehler

Swords
Page - Andriyko Podil
Knight - Fas Khan
Queen - Charles Deluvio
King - Santi Vedri & Tingey Injury Law Firm
Ace - Ria Alfana
Two - Oliver Twist & Mutzii
Three - Wendy Scofield
Four - Daniele Levis-Pelusi
Five - Dominik Scyth
Six - Steve Douglas
Seven - Nick Karvounis
Eight - Mak
Nine - Bernard 3
Ten - Greg Evans

Wands
Page - Alexander Dummer
Knight - Janko Ferlic
Queen - Jai Hill
King - Ariel
Ace - Carlo Linares
Two - Dana Cristea
Three - Filip Mroz
Four - Murilo Viviani

```
Five - Annie Spratt
Six - Wan San Yip
Seven - Ayodeji Alabi
Eight - Kaung Myat-Min
Nine - Luiza Braun
Ten - Annie Spratt
```

Pentacles
```
Page - Gift Habeshaw
Knight - Arseny Togulev
Queen - Karl Frederckson
King - Henley Design Studio
Ace - Camila Waz
Two - Alexey Turenko
Three - Robert Collins
Four - Mitchell Luo
Five - Casey Horner & Muhammad Muzamil
Six - Andriyko Podil
Seven - Christian Bowen
Eight - This is Engineering Raeng Q
Nine - Senjuti Kundu
Ten - Arif Riyanto
```

Cups
```
Page - Clarene Lalata & Clarissa Carbun
Knight - Annie Spratt
Queen - Yehor milohrods
King - Luke Michael & Paul Hanaoka
Ace - Jelleke Vanooteghem
Two - Nathan Dumlao
Three - Pablo Merchan-Montes
Four - Artem Beliaikin
Five - Nomao Saeki
Six - Chris Jarvis
Seven - Eric Prouzet & Mariana Dal Chic
Eight - Nrd
Nine - Sidney Pearce
Ten - Jonathan Borba
```

About the Author

Emily Paper grew up in Ontario, Canada and spent much of her time in solitude seeking mystical inspiration. Credit for her Hermit-like intuitive development goes to her parents, who often sent the kids deep into the woods assuming they could survive on their own. They almost all did!

After completing an undergraduate degree in Psychology from the University of Waterloo, she moved to the United States and studied Technical Writing while working in both high-tech industry and educational nonprofit organizations. She published online technical articles, wrote a few murder mystery drafts, and settled into a stable job in technical support.

Everything was fine, then suddenly a pandemic!

During the shutdown, Emily returned to her childhood passion for claircognizance and solitude, obtained certification in Feng Shui, and started Tarot and runic consulting.

Today, she is a divination and Feng Shui specialist, but with over 35 years of random fortune telling experience, it took losing a set of car keys to inspire her to write a book about it.

Emily lives in Washington State with her husband, and any money they earn goes straight to the college bursar's office for their three studious children.

Emily can be found wandering around social media, and at www.emilypaper.com

Coming in 2021 from Applied Divination

Applied Runes

An Excessively Practical Guide to Rune Interpretations

What movie should you watch when you pull a Naudiz / Nyd rune?

What about the Truman Show?!

Frankly, everyone should just watch the Truman Show, anyway. It is good.

Follow emilypaper.com for more information.

www.ingramcontent.com/pod-product-compliance
Lightning Source LLC
LaVergne TN
LVHW051544070426
835507LV00021B/2400